an

Bicultural and Trilingual Education:
The Foyer Model in Brussels

MULTILINGUAL MATTERS

MULTILINGUAL MATTERS 54
Series Editor: Derrick Sharp

Bicultural and Trilingual Education: The Foyer Model in Brussels

Edited by
Michael Byram and Johan Leman

MULTILINGUAL MATTERS LTD
Clevedon - Philadelphia

NB. The programme analysed here received financial support from the Commission of the European Communities within the framework of the action programme of 9-2-1976. The opinions expressed in this book are the sole responsibility of the authors themselves.

Library of Congress Cataloging in Publication Data
Bicultural and trilingual education
  (Multilingual matters; 54)
  Bibliography: p.
  Includes index.
  1. Education, Bilingual—Belgium—Brussels—Case studies. 2. Intercultural education—Belgium—Brussels—Case studies. 3. Multilingualism—Belgium—Brussels—Case studies. I. Byram, Michael. II. Leman, J., 1946-   .
III. Series: Multilingual matters (Series); 54.
LC3736.B42B783   1989   371.97′09493′3   88-34562

British Library Cataloguing in Publication Data
Bicultural and trilingual education: The Foyer model in Brussels
  (Multilingual matters: 54).
  1. Belgium. Brussels. Immigrant children.
  Education
  I. Byram, Michael II. Leman, Johan
  371.97′009493′3

ISBN 1-85359-044-4
ISBN 1-85359-043-6 pbk

Multilingual Matters Ltd

Bank House, 8a Hill Road   &   1900 Frost Road, Suite 101
Clevedon, Avon BS21 7HH   Bristol, PA 19007
England   U.S.A.

Index compiled by Meg Davies (Society of Indexers)
Typeset by Proteus, Worle, Avon
Printed and bound in Great Britain by WBC Print, Bristol

For all the pupils and teachers
of Foyer Model schools

Contents

Preface

The following pages constitute a description and evaluation of the Foyer Model of bicultural education at its present state of development. There are of course many models of bilingual and bicultural education throughout the world, each of which is interesting in itself, and each of which is doubtless unique to its own situation. Certainly, the context of the Foyer Model — in the officially bilingual but in fact multilingual city of Brussels — is unique. And the Foyer Model reflects its context in its aim of creating the conditions for children to become bicultural and trilingual. Nonetheless, it is only the detailed study of individual cases that provides the basis for more wide-ranging theorising and generalisation. And it is in the description of the experience of those involved that other practitioners may find solace and insight for their own problems and situations.

These are some of the reasons why it was decided to publish a book on the Foyer in English, making it more accessible to a wide audience. Other aspects of the work will appear in a companion volume in French, *Vivre l'interculturel. Les projets d'enseignement biculturel du Foyer à Bruxelles*, edited by J. Leman, to be published in 1989 by De Boeck of Brussels. It will deal specifically with the *intercultural* elements in the bicultural and trilingual Foyer projects in Brussels. M. Byram will analyse the nature of cultural learning and develop an argument based on theories of language and culture acquisition in mono-lingual and monocultural children. M. Danesi will study interculturalism as it is experienced by trilingual Italian children. J.A. Fernández de Rota and M. del Pilar will consider the intercultural relationships in the Spanish project in detail. L. Marchi will discuss the reciprocal perceptions and attitudes between Italian, Spanish, Turkish, and Moroccan parents and Belgian parents. K. Snoeck will deal with interculturalism in the Turkish project. L. Smeekens will discuss structural aspects. J. Leman, finally, will situate the intercultural facets of the projects in the global multicultural context of Brussels. In this volume the authors concentrate mainly on linguistic issues and on the structure, history and future of the Model as a means of providing a good education for immigrant children within the existing school system.

Practitioners — whether teachers, supervisors or administrators — are inevitably the ones who suffer the requests of researchers for information, opinions and plans for the future. Their names do not appear in the list of contributors; yet they are constantly present in these pages. The thanks of all the contributors are due, and it is the pleasure of the editors to make those thanks explicit, and to remind readers that the everyday joys and tribulations of the Foyer Model schools are not forgotten by those who have had the privilege of working with them.

Support for the work of the Foyer has been provided by the Directorate-General 5 of the European Economic Community and the Foyer wishes to express its gratitude here, as well as to Professor Serena Di Carlo for her stimulating assistance.

Introduction

MICHAEL BYRAM and JOHAN LEMAN

The immediate origin of this book lies in the process of evaluation of the Foyer Model which took place in 1986 and 1987. The majority of the contributions are based on evaluation reports written for Foyer, which is a non-state organisation concerned with the well-being of immigrants and their children in Brussels. Foyer had established a special programme for immigrant children in a number of Dutch-speaking schools in Brussels. In order to obtain a full and disinterested evaluation of its work after six years of development, Foyer commissioned a number of evaluations on an international level. Once these evaluations were complete, it was evident that, in an amended form, they would be of interest to others with similar concerns. So often, evaluation reports remain unpublished, because of their very nature as internal documents, when they might be made accessible to a wider audience after a little re-writing. In this case it was decided to use the opportunity to make them accessible to an even wider audience by publishing in English.

Evaluation

The process of evaluation is an important one, and should ideally be part of the planning from the beginning of such projects. Evaluation has to be seen not in terms of final judgements but as the opportunity to take stock. It is the chance for those involved to see themselves mirrored in the eyes and instruments of the evaluators but it is also the occasion for independent reflection. How, then, was this done in the case of the Foyer Model?

In the course of the sixth year of operation, in which the first group of pupils was completing its sixth and last year of bicultural primary education, several external evaluations were performed. The first, global evaluation was done by the European Community, which had accepted the Model and its individual projects as a pilot project, and was conducted by Professor Serena

Di Carlo of the University of Perugia in Italy. However, this evaluation, both as regards its purpose and its publication, is under the authority of the European Community supervisory agencies. Because the Foyer wanted to have a number of specific research questions examined in detail, contact was made with external evaluators to whom very specific questions were submitted. The responses were to be cast in the form of texts that could serve as the basis for modification of the projects by the Foyer.

The first important question was submitted to Professor G. Extra of the 'Werkverband Taal en Minderheden' of the Faculty of Letters of the Katholieke Universiteit Brabant in Tilburg, The Netherlands. He was asked to have his Centre make a study of the concrete acquisition of Dutch in the projects in order to see where and how it could, in his opinion, be improved.

Under the direction of Dr K. Jaspaert and Ms G. Lemmens, a year-long study of this language acquisition was carried out. It focused on the children of one of the Italian projects. Two research questions were posed:

— To what extent do the immigrant children of Italian origin master Dutch after participating in a bicultural educational programme in the primary school?

— What characteristics of the model could have influenced the result of the first part of the research question and how?

The 'Werkverband Taal en Minderheden' of Tilburg University considered the evaluation very interesting because of the specific multilingual context, among other reasons:

In general, it is difficult to isolate and measure the effects of second-language education in a context in which the language input comes from within and without the school. The effects of directed and spontaneous language acquisition are difficult to separate. Because the Dutch of these children is largely limited to the school environment, a research condition is present in which the role of the in-school language input in the development of skills in another language than the mother tongue can be better investigated (Lemmens Jaspaert, 1987:6).

In addition to the acquisition of Dutch, the Foyer is, of course, also interested in the acquisition of the mother tongue and in an evaluation of the concept of 'mother tongue' in the projects. To what extent is this still a 'mother tongue'? What is the status of the regional linguistic varieties, etc.? Because the most advanced group consists of Italian children, contact was made with Dr M. Danesi of the Department of Italian Studies of the University of Toronto in Canada. The choice of an Italian/Canadian evaluator was based on two considerations: first, the Canadian situation is similar in some respects to that of Brussels, and second, it could well be that the mother tongue of immigrant children could best be evaluated for its proper value and merit by someone who has had specific experience with the immigrant situation.

Because another well advanced group consisted of Spanish children and because the Foyer preferred not to limit its evaluations to one subgroup and school, J.A. Fernández de Rota y Monter, Professor of Social Anthropology at the University of Santiago in Spain, and Dr M. del Pilar Irimia Fernández, Head of the Institute for Special Education 'Santiago Apóstol' in La Coruña, Spain, were asked to investigate two research questions:

— What does the bicultural project, respectively Spanish and the two other languages, Dutch and French, mean for the Spanish parents and children?

— What is the quality of the children's Spanish, with school situations in Spain being taken as a reference point, given that the most advanced Spanish project children still have one important year of bicultural education?

For the final external evaluation, Dr. M.S. Byram of the School of Education of the University of Durham, Great Britain, was approached. He was asked to evaluate the educational implications, possibilities and shortcomings of the bicultural educational project. The Foyer was of the opinion that an 'educational' evaluation would be concerned with the bicultural curriculum, its effects on the curriculum as a whole, the realisation of curriculum goals, and the participants' experience of the curriculum and the underlying policy. In addition, the Foyer asked that consideration be given to the project's impact on the school as a possible agent for change both of the school structure and the school culture in order to facilitate 'integration'. During a preliminary visit, Dr Byram and the Foyer agreed that a case study of one of the schools involved should have the following aims:

— describe and analyse the curriculum of the immigrant children;

— describe how the participants (children, teachers, parents) experience and perceive the curriculum of the immigrant children and how the teachers experience participation in the curriculum innovation;

— describe how Belgian participants (children, teachers, parents) experience and perceive the presence of immigrant children and their curriculum.

All the researchers agreed to evaluate the project. Very useful evaluation reports were produced which, together with the evaluation report of Professor

Di Carlo, form excellent basic texts for the Foyer in the further development of the projects in the coming years. The researchers' texts published here are based on their participation in one or more of the bicultural educational projects. They are supplemented by a number of chapters written by members of the staff of the Foyer: L. Marchi, L. Smeekens, K. Snoeck, who also worked with the data of H. Desmedt and E. Redant, and J. Leman. The staff members report on aspects with which they have been involved every day for these six years.

The chapters which follow are largely concentrated on the linguistic development of the pupils in Foyer Model schools. This was the principal concern of the researchers and it is the question which most parents and teachers ask first. Yet the Model is not just bilingual or even trilingual; it is above all bicultural. There are therefore constant references to the general sociocultural development of pupils and the context in which they live.

In the first chapter, Leman describes the history of the Foyer Model as a response to the specific problems of immigrants in Brussels. It is here that the rationale for the instrumental use of immigrant languages, for the introduction of intercultural education and for the pursuit of trilingualism is explained. In the second chapter Jaspaert and Lemmens direct their attention to the all-important question of whether immigrant children can cope with adding Dutch to their repertoire of languages. Teachers and parents have followed their intuitions and trusted in the opinions and experience of themselves and Foyer for a number of years. The vindication of their trust is the focus of this second chapter.

In Chapter 3, one of the Foyer staff, Loredana Marchi, explains the linguistic rationale for the Foyer Model in greater detail by describing language changes among Italian immigrants. In accounting for change in terms of creativity rather than interference from one language to another, she argues that such change is the basis for 'linguistic mobility', for the ability to use the full repertoire available to all immigrants but especially children. Linguistic mobility itself is fundamental to a harmonious balance between integration and separation. In the next chapter, Danesi examines one aspect of the repertoire more closely and speculates on the relationship between literacy in the immigrant language and the cognitive development of the pupils. He describes in some detail his collection of a corpus of language and draws upon the well established work in North America to evaluate the effects of the Foyer Model. In Chapter 5, Byram discusses the question of children's and parents' identity as revealed in interviews with Italian informants. The well-known phenomenon of intended but seldom realised return to the country of origin is, it is argued, a vital part of and support for ethnic identity.

Chapter 6 moves the focus to Spanish children in another project. Rota y Monter and Pilar compare the children's language development in Spanish with two groups of children in Spain. They were, however, also interested in the general question of the integration of the children in the school as a whole. A particularly interesting part of their study concerns Spanish pupils' perceptions of the identity of 'Belgians' and of another immigrant group, the 'Moroccans'. Chapter 7 deals with a third project and a group of children who are not as far advanced in the Model as the Italians or the Spaniards. Snoeck investigated the issue of teaching mathematics, with reference to Turkish children. The use of the 'mother tongue' for teaching mathematics in the first year of primary school is one which has much exercised all those involved in the Foyer projects. Snoeck discusses the particular problems, both linguistic and cultural, of Turkish children and suggests some of the implications for teaching.

Chapters 8 and 9 take us back to general theoretical issues in the Foyer Model. It has been axiomatic that children should be taught in part by teachers of the same origin as themselves in order to support their sense of identity. In Chapter 8, Byram discusses why this should be so in the theory developed in the Model and reflects on the extent to which it is realised in practice. Another axiom has been the need for projects to be integrated into and have influence upon the structures of the schools in which they are housed. Smeekens, drawing upon his experience of managing the growth of several projects, discusses how the process of curricular and structural innovation has taken place.

In the final chapter we draw up the balance as it stands at the moment. There are a number of questions arising out of experience so far which remain unresolved. Simultaneously the context in which Foyer works is constantly changing. Every extension to another school or another ethnic group brings new problems and new insights. Changes in patterns of immigration and settlement will require new responses and modifications to existing practices. And, not least in a country in which education is always a highly political issue, the attention of politicians to the educational needs of immigrants is becoming ever more evident.

We end therefore on the note already struck in our preface: this volume is not a definitive account of the Foyer Model. It is a collection of views of the Model in its current state of development which will, we hope, be of interest to all those involved in the constantly changing scene of education for minorities. Those constant changes necessitate constant vigilance and response. Immigration, settlement, integration, ethnic identity are dynamic processes. If there is one simple point to be made from the experience described in the following chapters, it is that our response must be equally dynamic.

Reference

LEMMENS G. and JASPAERT, K 1987, 'Evaluatie van het Nederlands in het Foyer bicultureel onderwijsproject'. Tilburg: Internal Foyer Report.

1 Multilingualism as Norm, Monolingualism as Exception: The Foyer Model in Brussels

JOHAN LEMAN

The Brussels Context

For the foreigner, Brussels is simply the capital of Belgium but from a Belgian perspective, and in particular for our purposes here, it is necessary to make some finer distinctions. Unless otherwise stated the agglomeration of Brussels is understood here as consisting of 19 Brussels municipalities of which the city of Brussels itself constitutes only one municipal district (see map).

Immigrants from the Mediterranean live mostly in the central districts of Brussels, namely in the heart of Brussels city and in the older working class neighbourhoods of St.-Gillis, Anderlecht, St.-Jans-Molenbeek, Koekelberg, Schaarbeek and St.-Joost-ten-Noode. Other foreigners, financially better placed and who cannot be classified as immigrant workers, live in the residential suburbs east and south of the agglomeration of which St.-Pieters-Woluwe and Ukkel are prime examples. In the municipalities of Vorst, Elsene, Etterbeek and the district of Laken belonging to the city of Brussels, both types of foreigners can be found on a fairly mixed basis: both the mediterranean immigrant seeking social promotion for himself and his family along with the less well-off foreigner who does not belong to the class of immigrant workers. The five existing bicultural projects in 1987–88 are situated in the city of Brussels (2), a working class district of Anderlecht (1) and St.-Jans-Molenbeek (1) and the neighbourhood of Laken (1) belonging to the city of Brussels. Extensions to take place in September 1988 are planned for Schaarbeek (1), St.-Joost-ten-Noode (1), Jette (1) and possibly Etterbeek (1).

7

THE AGGLOMERATION OF BRUSSELS
(source: *Brussel doorgelicht*. Agglomeratie Brussel 1986)

If we consider the figures for each population category as shown by the latest census (1981) we can draw the following conclusions. In 1981 the agglomeration of Brussels consisted of 997,293 inhabitants of which 759,418 were Belgians and 237,875 foreigners (23.85%). Remarkably large groups were the Moroccans (57,874), the Italians (35,809), the Spaniards (28,156), the Turks (15,820) and the Greeks (9,629). Other groups were not so numerous. Another kind of foreigner, considered as being less 'foreign' by the native inhabitants, was the non-mediterraneans, namely the French (25,759), the Britons (7,005) and the Dutch (4,566). In 1985, despite the increasing number of naturalisations, there were 248,131 foreigners in Brussels.

Naturalisations apart, the number of inhabitants of Belgian origin in Brussels can be estimated at 600,000. To this must be added another 300,000 to 350,000 foreigners and 'new' Belgians who are largely the immigrant workers who have established themselves here on a permanent basis. This is a 2:1 ratio. In certain districts more than 50% of the inhabitants are of mediterranean origin and their children make up 80 to 90% or more of the kindergarten and primary school population in these areas. Throughout the agglomeration 50% of new-born children are of foreign origin.

Thus we can conclude that a first major characteristic of the situation in Brussels is its very high concentration of foreigners.

A second feature concerns the native Belgian population. Here we have to take into account that Brussels is a bilingual city with both French and Dutch as official languages. Most Belgian people in Brussels have some knowledge of both languages although there is a greater proficiency in French. Others speak only one language. In an introduction to bicultural education projects for immigrant children in Brussels it is not our aim to discuss the complicated issue of the Dutch versus French speaking population in the capital. However, in order to get an idea about the figures involved, it is estimated that about 20% (perhaps more) of the population is Dutch-speaking and 50% French-speaking. Alongside these groups we also have the 30% foreigners and 'new' Belgians. For these people the language they speak within the home — usually a dialect originating from their home country moulded by French influences — differs from the language they use in the wider society, which is usually French. This makes the French language a dominant force in public life.

Despite this the Dutch language has gained considerably in importance over the last few years. There are two reasons for this. Firstly the demand has increased for bilingual employees in trade and industry, along with the need for English in the more qualified professions. Secondly, proficiency in the Dutch language has become a way of distinguishing people as 'non-foreign' or integrated. Employers demand people with a knowledge of both languages. This is not surprising, considering Brussels is economically and geographically closer to the Dutch-speaking northern part of Belgium. It is precisely this part that has prospered demographically and economically over the last decades in comparison with its French-speaking southern counterpart.

Because of its ethnic-cultural and linguistic complexities, with both its synchronic as well as diachronic aspects, the Brussels situation is a unique and extremely fascinating field in which to work. It poses a real challenge for the development of an educational pedagogy for immigrant children, especially when one takes into account the following seven points: the actual family situation; the predominant street image; the real employment possibilities; the educational opportunities for the child if its parents decide to go back to their homeland; the child's cultural rights; other arguments, both sociolinguistic and socio-affective, in favour of an efficient development of the language of origin; and last but not least the ever-growing reality of Brussels as a yet more complex, multicultural and multilingual European city.

One can hardly place the respective languages of Brussels immigrant families on the same level as that of standard languages. They are either a substandard language, or a dialect (morphologically sometimes differing considerably from the standard language), or a mixed language, or — in some cases — French.

The street image is predominantly French and often (but not always) it becomes the first socialisation language of the children involved. However, one cannot disregard the fact already stated earlier that the typical Belgian bilingualism (French/Dutch) is becoming increasingly important as far as public services, supermarkets, etc. are concerned. In a way, the lesser known Dutch language has developed into a kind of selective force. This also becomes apparent when one starts looking for a house to rent and so on. Dutch and French are the two principal national Belgian languages, both within the capital and the country as a whole, and both vie for status in Brussels with varying degrees of success.

The Foyer's Aims

The Foyer is a socio-pedagogical centre for the reception and guidance of immigrants and their children in Brussels.

The Foyer Model, which functions at the kindergarten and primary school level of the Dutch education system in Brussels, essentially aims to turn the apparent confusion of divergent and sometimes contradictory language stimuli, which is specific to the Brussels situation, into an advantage for the child by means of an adequate structuring of his/her reception within the school.

We can also point out that primary education in Dutch-speaking schools in Brussels enjoys a particularly favourable teacher–pupil ratio, owing to the fact that an average class numbers about fifteen pupils.

When the Project was conceived in 1981 five objectives were set forth. We discuss them in their initial form. At its outset the Project aimed to influence the children, their parents and families, the teachers and the school as a whole. The objectives were:

a. For children and teachers: learning to live together in a complex, multicultural society.

Although the Foyer Model is initially directed to the needs of immigrant pupils in school, the 'ordinary' education of native pupils can also be influenced by its method and by the school as an organisation. In this way a step is made towards a true 'encounter education', as the initiative is called by the Flemish-Belgian Ministry of Education. The school can best prepare the pupils (native and foreign) for life in a multicultural society by allowing them to discover for themselves in their own school the problems and the possibilities of such a society.

b. For immigrant children: the acquisition of very good trilingualism by the end of primary school.

In view of their future opportunities in Brussels, we attach great importance to fluency in Dutch and French for immigrant children. The model as a whole covers a period of nine years in the life of the immigrant child: three years of kindergarten and six years of primary school. The purpose of the bicultural kindergarten is firstly to provide a very good preparation for the primary school. The next objective is to improve the linguistic skills in the mother tongue of the child so that the first primary year can be commenced on an adequate level. Finally, the child is introduced to Dutch in the kindergarten.

While reading and writing are taught in the language of origin throughout the first primary year, familiarity with Dutch is also promoted, taking advantage of their very young age. As far as possible, Dutch is presented not only as a 'cultural language' but primarily as a living 'communication language'. During the second primary year the language of origin, the 'mother tongue', is worked on further. But, at the same time, the children are immersed in Dutch and are taught a new, Dutch, writing code.

In the meantime, most of the children have acquired a smattering of French as a third language, generally as a result of TV and street encounters and sometimes as a fragmentary home language, if it was not already for many of them their first socialisation language. During the third primary year and in the years that follow, while the 'mother tongue' is further built on and Dutch is activated as the language of education and integration, the third written code,

French, is introduced. From this point on it is taught systematically with the same intensity as it is with Flemish children.

At the end of the six years of primary school, these children should be completely trilingual, without the danger of 'semilingualism'. This increases their real chances for integration in Brussels and in Belgium and will prevent them from being robbed of their cultural identity in the Belgian context. Obviously this cannot be accomplished during the first two or three years of primary education. This is a programme that extends over the six years of primary education with, if possible, an adequate kindergarten curriculum as its foundation. In addition it requires increased personal effort on the part of all the teachers involved.

c. For immigrant children and their families: enhanced opportunities for integration in their country of origin should their parents decide to return.

We have just noted that the opportunities for integration in the host country are enhanced. The particular structure of the school model with its provision for education in the mother tongue also safeguards these same opportunities for integration in the country of origin, should schooling be prematurely interrupted by the parents' decision to return to their homeland.

d. For schools: maintenance of and possible improvement in the level of quality.

With its bicultural projects the Foyer has clearly in mind the advancement of the immigrant child. For the Foyer, it is obvious that the school should be requested, if not required, to do everything possible to raise the quality of its education to as high a level as possible, in order to develop the special nature of each child, native as well as foreign. Certainly more effort is demanded from the teachers in the projects, but it could be that these efforts are easier to make within the meaningful context of the projects themselves.

e. For immigrant parents and their families: closer involvement in the school and in their children's socialisation within it and thereby increased participation in social life and in the wider society.

It might seem surprising that the Foyer also sees its bicultural projects as an appropriate initiative for the structured integration of parents, or perhaps, a structured resident participation in an urban multicultural society. For the Foyer, it has always been clear that not too many demands may be made of the school and that the school alone is not capable of accomplishing integration. A school is one such factor, but working with adults is certainly desirable, at least in the Foyer model and within the typical Brussels situation of the Dutch-language school system. As far as possible, we try to unite the parents in a parents' committee.

We can conclude that in line with the primary objectives of this initiative and with the specific teacher–pupil ratios in Dutch-speaking schools in Brussels we opt for one project, with one nationality, in one school. This leads to different projects within a *bicultural* model. These projects are elaborated with an *intercultural* perspective in which we opt for *trilinguality* in the children involved. Inherent in the model is the stimulation of the participation of the immigrant *parents* in the school life.

In our opinion, the Foyer experiment is set in historic circumstances ideal for achieving its objectives. In Belgian education, because of the fall in the birth rate, there are more school places than students. The lack of students is, it would appear, especially significant in Dutch speaking schools in Brussels. These are the city's élitist schools, who feel they can cover their vacancies by attracting the children of immigrants. In this way they will be filling a social need and, of course, they could not justifiably exclude such students. (J.A. Fernández de Rota and M. del Pilar, 1987: 10).

The Foyer Model

The model that was applied in the beginning, in 1981, was an adapted version of a model that has been in use for some time in Leiden (Holland). The model is one of gradual integration with as much importance as possible being given to the preservation and reinforcement of the pupil's cultural identity. It is for this reason that a number of basic subjects are taught in the language of the group to which the child belongs, even though it might already have learned one of the national languages (generally French up to a certain, limited, level).

The prototype model is composed as follows:

Kindergarten period (three years)
1st year: 50% of the time as an ethnic group, separate, 50% together with native or other children.
2nd year: same.
3rd year: same.
Primary school period (six years)
1st year: About 60% as an ethnic-cultural group, separate (own language and culture + mathematics).
                  About 30% in Dutch as a 'new language', separate.
                  About 10% in integration activities, together with native or other children.
2nd year: About 50% as an ethnic-cultural group, separate (own language and culture, but no mathematics).

About 20% in Dutch as a 'new language', separate.

About 30% in integration activites + mathematics; in the course of the year, this 30% increases depending on the progress of the immigrant pupils, with the foreign teachers helping and supporting the children in this transition as much as possible.

3rd year on: 90% of the time all the children are taught together in Dutch. Three to four hours per week of instruction in the mother tongue, a few hours per week of instruction in French.

Initially the children are organised in separate classes, both in kindergarten and in primary school. In these classes, the core curriculum is taught in their own language of origin, and gradually they are introduced to Dutch at a time that is considered the most 'rewarding' for the child. How the prototype model will be adapted to each ethnic subgroup, and in particular to the Moroccan immigrant children among whom the language situation is rather complex, will be discussed separately.

In the second primary year, mathematics is already taught together with the Belgian children.

From the third primary year onwards, the children are completely integrated into the Dutch-language class. In the meantime, they continue to receive lessons in their mother tongue and, like their Belgian classmates, lessons in French.

Both in kindergarten and in the first two classes of primary school, the mother tongue is taught by full-time foreign teachers, who take care of the subject 'mother tongue' (i.e. language as object and language as medium) and who are part of the team of teachers. From the third class on, the mother tongue is again taught by one and the same, i.e. a third foreign teacher.

This is in fact a model of positive-didactic discrimination in concrete terms.

Of course, it must be noted here that the development of a model for intercultural education is, of itself, a process: the model is, within the normative limits that are proper to the profile, continually subject to changes and adjustments. Moreover, each individual school has its own needs. Every school is different and account must be taken of this in the implementation of a model. The model must be sufficiently flexible to be able to include within itself this 'individuality'.

With Which Ethnic Minorities?

The first group of children to take part in the Project were Italian children from Laken (part of the city of Brussels) in September 1981.

Owing to various circumstances, we started with seven Italian (mostly Sicilian) children in the first year of primary school. In the following year the Project was extended to include a kindergarten and the parents were requested to let their children attend at least one or two years bicultural kindergarten.

In September 1982 another project was introduced, this time with Spanish children in a big school to which initially no kindergarten was attached. As a result of considerable persuasion on our part we obtained the insertion of one bicultural class (comparable to the third year of kindergarten) as an introduction to the bicultural curriculum in the primary school. There are now 23 children participating in the Italian project and 12 in the first year of the Spanish project.

Both these projects took place within schools that had no previous contact with immigrant children. Into such a school, where the average class numbers between 10 and 15 children, the idea was to include about eight immigrant children each year, a few less than the number of native children per class. Each year these immigrant children, along with the project, move one step upwards within the structure of the school.

When planning the Project it was assumed that Italian and Spanish children would be most easily accepted by the Dutch-speaking schools in Brussels which have neither a tradition of absorbing immigrant children nor had been made aware by the Flemish-Brussels authorities of the possibility that such a high percentage (50%) of foreign births could or should lead to such a proposal. For years the Dutch-language schools had been attracting French-speaking children who had one parent or grandparent of Flemish origin, but no foreigners. The Foyer planned to follow up this Italian and Spanish project with a similar one for Turkish and Moroccan children.

But the first new demand came from a school in a working class area of Anderlecht which had offered places to 20 Italian immigrant children of varying ages without having access to a particular method or policy. It was thus decided to start a project here, too, beginning with the youngest children. Consequently we started, in September 1983, a second Italian project. This was a school with few Dutch-speaking children and a relatively high number of French-speaking Belgian children and children of mixed marriages (foreigner/Belgian). This proved later to be no easy basis on which to develop our usual method of work. At that time, in September 1983, there were already

36 Italian children involved in the first Italian project, 31 Spanish children in the Spanish project, and 22 Italian infants from the first three years of kindergarten participated in the second Italian project. In September 1984 the Foyer made the setting up of a Turkish and Moroccan project a priority. The resistance shown by the schools towards the inclusion of these two populations in such a project was striking. Eventually two state schools agreed to accept one project each and Turkish and Moroccan children respectively were accepted into their kindergarten.

Initially the Turkish project with its 20 Turkish toddlers encountered no specific problems. The Moroccan project in St.-Gillis was cancelled by the school management after a few days owing to protests from a handful of French and Dutch-speaking Belgian parents against its implementation and the presence of the Moroccan children in the school. Against the will of the Foyer as Project promoter and completely disregarding previously made agreements, the school handed the Moroccan children over to a small, remote district department to deal with. For one year the Moroccan children were looked after as well as possible by the Foyer and afterwards entrusted to another school. Thus a first attempt to set up a Moroccan bicultural project prematurely came to grief.

In September 1985 the four existing projects continued to develop still further. No new project was promoted because of the Foyer's decision to delay starting anything new until a Moroccan project was successfully off the ground. This only came about in September 1986 when the Foyer's fifth project was once again introduced into a kindergarten of an ordinary school in a working-class quarter of St.-Jans-Molenbeek. An agreement was reached between the Foyer and the school that the number of Moroccan children would never exceed more than one third of the total number of pupils in each year and that the Moroccan children were obliged to spend at least the first two years in the kindergarten.

By September 1987 310 immigrant children, spread throughout five schools, were participating in projects. One of these schools was a large, high quality institute which alongside the Spanish children also attracted pupils from élite Flemish families. The other four schools can be classified as of medium, or slightly lower, quality, but definitely not poor. One of these four schools was described in the following words by Byram and his words could reasonably be applied to all four.

The school has gone through a process of change independently of the introduction of the Project. On the one hand there are proportionately more pupils from lower social classes than five to ten years ago. On the other hand there has been an increase in children from French-speaking families, probably because parents realise the advantages for children of attaining proficiency in Dutch and also because they want to send their children to a school where there are fewer immigrant children, especially of Turkish and Moroccan origin. Italian children are not considered to lower the standards of a school in the same way as other immigrants.

These two factors — changes in social origins and the increased presence of French-speaking children — are likely to change the nature of the school and the degree to which it can attain the academic standards of the past. The well-established correlation between social class and academic attainment raises the expectation that attainment will fall as the school has a greater number of pupils from lower classes, whatever their linguistic or cultural origins. Similarly, it appears logical to expect that a greater proportion of French-speakers will affect the Dutch character of the school and, secondly, lower academic attainment, since more pupils are learning in a second language irrespective of their cultural background, be it Belgian or Italian. Whether these expectations are justified or whether they are self-fulfilling by creating the results they suggest, cannot be commented on here. The consequences are similar whatever the causal process. (Byram, 1987: 15–16).

At the time of writing, February 1988, a request has been made for a second Turkish project to be set up in Schaarbeek (and possibly another in St.-Joost-ten-Noode) and we are making inquiries into the possibility of setting up a second Moroccan project in Jette. While concrete arrangements have been made for the Turkish project to begin in September 1988 no clear details have emerged as regards the second Moroccan project. Both schools already contain Turkish and Moroccan children respectively. It is also worth mentioning that for the second time in the history of the projects contact has been made with another high quality Flemish-speaking school in Brussels (Etterbeek) over the possibility of starting a bicultural project with Turkish, Italian or Spanish children. The school directory board itself feels that in recognising the reality of Brussels as a multicultural city they must oppose the present tendency to regard the Dutch-language schools as 'only for white Belgian children' and the French-language schools as 'only for coloured children'. As a school they feel they must take up their responsibility in this matter, but the directory board wants the teachers to agree with this point of view before starting up the project.

So in September 1988 we look forward to an increase in the number of projects on offer . . .

The History of the Curriculum

The history of the curriculum followed by the Italian pioneer group is reconstructed from teachers' diaries and pupils' books as analysed in Byram's Evaluation Report (1987), and from observations made during the six years of guidance by Foyer workers.

The pioneer group made up of Italian children started without any bicultural kindergarten background and consisted partly of children who had attended a French-language kindergarten and partly of children who had been to a Dutch-speaking one.

In 1981–82 the Italian pioneer group (whose progress we monitor each year) was launched into the first year of primary school. During the lessons given in their mother tongue (940 minutes per week) they concentrated mainly on reading, writing and mathematics. Lessons given in Dutch (380 minutes per week) were oral and activity based (painting, making things, singing), where Dutch was used primarily as a medium but where additional opportunity was made for the teacher to point out the structures and vocabulary of the language. In both Italian and Dutch lessons the pupils acted linguistically as 'carriers' of culture, an important factor in the development of their social identity. The aim was to make Dutch seem less foreign and remote by using it for 'fun' subjects and at the same time ensuring that the first contact with the children of other languages took place in a particularly relaxing atmosphere, whereby it was assumed that this same affectionate bond with the Italian language would develop normally at home.

A few times a year the children were invited to spend a long weekend with Dutch-speaking families and their children living outside Brussels. In the view of the Foyer this served two purposes: on the one hand to make the children familiar with a completely Dutch-speaking milieu where Dutch was the only possible means of communication, and on the other hand to bring them into contact with open-minded Flemish families who clearly accepted the reality of a multicultural society. Taking language holidays in Dutch-speaking families living outside Brussels is still common practice within the projects, also with Spanish, Turkish and later Moroccan children. They are considered important, not least for the Flemish families who gain through this encounter a positive contact with immigrants in their own lives. These people mostly obtain their information on the developments in the immigration debate through the newspapers.

In 1982–83 lessons in Italian decreased to 460 minutes per week while lessons in Dutch increased to 745 minutes per week. Mathematics was given in Dutch. The project was now squarely confronted with the lack of adequate available textbook material in both Dutch and Italian. One cannot adopt a textbook from Italy without adapting it to the current situation. Nor is it advisable to transpose the Dutch curriculum onto Italian immigrant children without making the necessary adaptations. Ultimately, the Brussels situation differs from most of the others where education is given in a second language because of the strong presence of French, the language of the streets, both within the school among the Belgian (also Flemish) and Italian children, and also in the life of the immigrant children themselves. In practice it means production of new teaching materials, which take more than a year to produce, or a careful adaptation of L1 materials.

During the third year, 1983–84, Italian was reduced to four lessons and French was introduced by the Dutch teacher, who also taught all other subjects. French is no unknown quantity for these children in Brussels, nor indeed for the Belgian children. Even more so than for Dutch and Italian the 'French as a foreign language' textbooks are inappropriate, nor is it enough simply to modify their methodology. The curtailing of the Italian language is partly compensated for by the setting up of a leisure centred 'Club Italiano' outside school whose aim is to promote 'linguistic fluency' and an affective bond with the Italian language by means of Italian films, singing, theatre and, later on, computer-centred activities, all carried out in Italian.

The general pattern in the fourth year, 1984–85, was similar to that of the third year. The 'Club Italiano' continued to fulfil an important role in terms of 'linguistic fluency'. This provided important compensation since the affective dimension was given a smaller place in the overt Italian curriculum, although it remained present in the hidden curriculum at school, i.e. in teachers' attitudes and values transmitted to pupils. The function of spoken and written Italian in the life of these children, both the standard language and the non-standard variations of it, is dealt with in Danesi's contribution to this book. Here we need only note that the children are well aware of which form they speak in, and, for example, are able to identify the difference between the Italian and Sicilian languages when required, even though they tend to use Sicilian words in their everyday speech, something which rarely occurs in their written work. As regards Dutch, the children were further encouraged by their teacher to move away from a textbook use of the language. The development of Dutch within the Foyer model is dealt with in detail in the section of this book written by Jaspaert and Lemmens, and is discussed in great detail in their evaluation report (Lemmens & Jaspaert, 1987).

In 1985–86 and 1986–87, the fifth and sixth year, the curriculum did not differ essentially from the two previous years. Particular effort was required of the Belgian teacher during these two years not to present geography and history in simply a Belgium-centred way. History is particularly important because of its potential rôle in supporting the cultural identity. The effort that is required is really to treat history not from a Belgian point of view, nor even Belgian supplemented with a touch of Italian, but to deal with it essentially from a European perspective. Fluency in the Dutch language must be further worked on, while at the same time the children must be prepared in the grammatical and structural side of the language for their eventual entry, after the sixth year, into the secondary school. A good elementary basis of the Italian language was worked on to enable the children to communicate easily in Italian. In the third and fourth years a start had been made with a specific intercultural lesson given every two weeks. This is now further developed in a systematic way in the final two years, whereby respect for language, considering the children's proficiency in three of them, provides a good basis on which to work.

On considering the development of each class within every project, six years after the beginning of the first Italian project, one notices that almost all the pupils since then have attended kindergarten, which means they have a greater facility than the pioneer group in both Dutch and Italian at the beginning of the primary school. Dutch is therefore taught more as a second language than it was with the pioneer group. In the first year the same mathematics syllabus is taught to both immigrant and Dutch pupils, using the same 'new materials'. Out of the four projects we are considering for this purpose maths is taught in two of them in the mother tongue and in the other two in Dutch. It appears to make no difference for the children; progress in mathematics appears to be more influenced by the quality of the teacher and the individual capacity of the child than by whether it is taught in the mother tongue or in Dutch. The children themselves do not consider this an important factor : 'maths is maths' say the Italian and Spanish children. What does seem important is that if mathematics is taught in one language then the most important concepts dealt with should be taken up again during a lesson in the other language. Nevertheless, the whole issue must be further investigated, in conjunction with Turkish children for example, before further useful comment can be made on it. Our findings in this matter must be seen as tentative. Staff member K. Snoeck is studying in more detail the question of mathematics.

Lessons of a more 'fun' nature and sometimes also those with a potentially culture-specific content (drawing, craft, music, current affairs) continue to be mainly, but not exclusively, in Dutch. This choice was made because of the fact that the structural anchorage of the project, i.e. the importance given to the place of the mother tongue within the school, is more secured by the crediting of the so-called 'important' subjects (reading, writing, mathematics) to the mother tongue during the first years of the curriculum, than by the affective bond with the mother tongue pursued via the culturally sensitive but so-called 'less important' lessons at school.

This essentially has to do with the particular multicultural profile of the school promoted in Brussels. At the same time the Foyer reasons that the affective component in the relationship with the mother tongue is compensated for within the family, in which Dutch plays no part, and through a few stimulating, imaginative extra-curricular activities for the immigrant children, to which the native children are often invited. In 1987–88, for example, all children worked on the production of a multicultural musical outside school hours. The extra-school 'play' and 'fantasy stimulating' activities in the mother tongue take place from the third year onwards, at the same time that the use of the mother tongue within the school curriculum itself is proportionally curtailed.

From Byram's classroom observations of one Italian project we can draw on the following remarks, although we must not lose sight of the fact that throughout the project a number of completely normal processes run their usual course, as in every school.

The first and most important impression is that the school is like any other primary school in providing a secure and pleasant atmosphere for young children, with teachers who are concerned with them above all as children, then as pupils who are expected to learn and finally as pupils in a special project. This impression arises out of watching and listening to teachers working with children and from conversations with teachers themselves. That this is a Dutch-speaking school surrounded by a French-dominated environment is also as noticeable a part of the school ethos, as is its special nature as an experimental project school (Byram, 1987 : 29).

These remarks apply to all the other Project schools involved.

At the end of the sixth year of primary school the pioneer group itself, together with its Belgian classmates, spent a week in a fifth class, the last year of the 'scuola elementare' in Sicily. It proved to be a very interesting week for both the Italian and the Belgian children.

A few months later this first group made the step away from the Project into a Dutch-speaking secondary school. This step has not created any particular problems. The integration within the different schools the children now attend has been very positively handled.

Parents, Pupils and Teachers

The children discussed here are not isolated individuals. They are part of a history.

A differentiated picture must be drawn of the dynamic sociocultural praxis in the Brussels immigrant community. It varies depending on whether the people involved are first-, second-, or third-generation immigrants, on whether the point at issue is cultural and social creativity or deculturation (cf. Leman, 1987a), or on whether one is considering Italian (Sicilian), Spanish, Turkish or Moroccan parents or children. All of this would lead us too far afield, so I will limit myself here to the linguistic aspects of the people involved in the projects. I would again also stress that everything is presently taking place in an environment that has been strongly permeated by French.

The Italian and Spanish parents have three reasons for placing their children in a bicultural educational project. Many of them consider it important for their child to know the language of their country of origin in view of a possible return to the home country or because of family ties there and vacation visits to them. Most of these parents are first-generation immigrants. A number of people are also of the opinion that the children should know the language of their parents, even without an explicit reference to the country of origin. The mother tongue is thus the cultural link between the children and the parents. Finally, some parents consider the languages of themselves valuable, Spanish as a world language and Italian as the language of a great culture.

The tie with the mother tongue is perhaps the strongest among the Turkish parents, but the motivations are less differentiated.

Among the Moroccan parents, the language situation is the most complex. In Morocco itself, one may speak of diglossia between the modern standard Arabic, which differs little from classical Arabic of the Koran, and Moroccan Arabic, which is considered a dialect. Both languages are used by the same person in very specific situations. The sociolinguistic context determines the choice between the two languages. Modern standard Arabic is very important because of its national and religious significance, but not ethnic significance, for there the difference between dialectical Moroccan and Berber prevails. This situation must be both stressed and qualified: standard Arabic predominates in education but openness to a foreign language (particularly French) is rarely contested, not even in education. This complexity is present to a considerable extent in the mentality of the Moroccan immigrants in Brussels. The importance of standard Arabic, which cannot be called a mother tongue but rather a dominant school language, is 'national' and particularly 'religious'.

But which language is actually spoken at home? The chapter by Loredana Marchi in this book describes a number of striking aspects of the use of the mother tongue among Italian immigrant parents in the bicultural projects. Similar mechanisms operate among the first-generation Spanish and Turkish immigrants. Among the Moroccan parents, the linguistic usage is more complex because a number of them speak Berber and because of a still more explicit presence of French in some families.

Typical for the second-generation parents in Brussels, moreover, is the increasing prevalence of the use of French.

If we were to risk constructing a typology of the complex domestic use of languages in immigrant families in Brussels, two aspects must be emphasised. First, a lexical and particularly a morphological impoverishment occurs, that is, an intermingling of elements of the dialect of origin and the language of the host country in the various languages, combined with pidgin formation. Second, language mixing occurs with insufficient system separation. The parents speak their own language between themselves, albeit with the influences just noted, e.g. Frenchified Sicilian. Another language is sometimes used by the parents with their children, e.g. Sicilianised French. The children among themselves communicate still differently, e.g. in French or Dutch. Furthermore, the upward language, from the children to the parents, can have its own pattern. Such language mixing can also take on specific shadings when visitors are present.

As for why immigrant parents decide to enrol their children in a bicultural project, we note that these parents generally consider the cultural identity of origin important and/or want to make a material social step forward, at least initially. Specific significance is given to Dutch mostly by second-generation parents, who themselves sometimes have better command of French than the mother tongue. It is as though they want to give a new impetus to their stagnated immigrant situation. These parents have dropped the idea of returning to the country of origin and do not experience the mother tongue as a link between them and their children. They still continue to consider Spanish as a world language or Italian as a major cultural language, but they have in mind primarily a status enhancement for their children by enrolment, via a bicultural project, in Dutch-language education in Brussels. The mother tongue, nevertheless, is experienced as a closer bond between the family and the Dutch-language school.

Finally, there is bicultural education in families in which the husband and wife differ in their views of the future. For example, when one of the parents is a first-generation immigrant and the other a second-generation immigrant, it can happen that the former still dreams of returning to the home country while the latter does not at all. The bicultural model for their children, as conceived in Brussels, gives them time to resolve their conflict or at least not to make an over-hasty decision.

These considerations are those of the parents, but, in fact, the children are the ones who actually participate in the projects and live with the results. This book is primarily concerned with the question of what the projects mean for them, socially, culturally and linguistically. Danesi discusses the Italian, and J. A. Fernández de Rota and Maria del Pilar Irimia Fernández the Spanish, of the children in the Project. Their acquisition of Dutch is examined by Jaspaert and Lemmens.

Although it is not my intention here to discuss the knowledge of the 'mother tongue' of these children, I do want to note in passing that, however broken they seem to have spoken it for a long time, the mother tongue arouses clear resonances among these children that are related to their home lives and this in a way that cannot be obtained by the school language. When the Italian (Sicilian) children were presented with a number of projective pictures of the world of adults, of their peers, the school, the family, the nuclear family, and themselves with the request to make up a story about them in Italian and Dutch, it was obvious how language and imagination are intensely linked to each other. While the mother tongue arouses resonances that are related to the real and vital home environment, the school language, here Dutch, generated a much more formal, less truly lived, and more external story (Leman, 1987b). We see in this an important argument for assigning a prominent role to education in the mother tongue, even though the child initially does less well in it, particularly in kindergarten and in the first years of primary school.

As regards the Belgian children, the effort is expressly made that they remain more numerous in each school than the immigrant children. Ghetto schools for foreign children are avoided. The effort is also made to allow these Belgian children the opportunity several times a week to learn their own mother tongue, here Dutch (but there are also many French-speaking Belgian children in Dutch-language education in Brussels) on their own level.

The last parties involved in the projects are the teachers, both Belgian and foreign. A number of foreign teachers were made available by foreign embassies, and some were recruited directly by the Foyer, particularly for the kindergarten classes. As for the Belgian teachers, in each school the teaching staff reflects the prevailing social concepts among the teachers in general. No special recruitment was done for the Project. This means that each school can have teachers who definitely support the Project objectives, others who have no explicit opinion on the matter, and still others who doubt the utility of a bicultural project. We consider it important in this discussion that the teachers be positive or at least neutral toward the Project, particularly in kindergarten and the first three years of primary school. Since Belgian teachers are legally dependent on their own educational authority, which is not the Project promoter and which can belong to one of three different Belgian educational systems (the free Catholic system, the municipal system, and the state system) and since the foreign teachers are dispatched by different foreign embassies while the Foyer, as the Project promoter, has no specific legal authority, the introduction of a bicultural project in a school naturally is a complex innovation process that must be started from the beginning each time. This is discussed by Smeekens elsewhere in this volume.

Some General Cultural-Anthropological Considerations

From the outset of the bicultural educational projects, the Foyer has considered it important to have a theoretical framework within which the bicultural projects could be interpreted. This theoretical framework would serve as a kind of horizon from which the functioning of the various aspects of the projects could be illuminated and adjusted. Conversely, the theoretical framework should be adapted as the projects develop in their diversity and complexity. Thus, nuances and adaptations have had to be made within the theoretical framework as it was described in 1983 and 1985 (Leman, 1983, 1985). Now, three years later, new additions are necessary. Nevertheless, the basic tenets have remained the same over the years, and are summarised here.

a. A view of society in Brussels

Brussels has become *de facto* a multicultural and multilingual city, even more than previously. At the same time, Brussels is destined to become the capital of an ever more united Europe. The reduction of the discussion of Brussels to a discussion between Dutch-speaking and French-speaking Belgians will in time be overtaken by events. Other languages, because they are spoken by representative groups of Europeans living in Brussels, will be able to claim a rightful place in Europe's capital. I have in mind Spanish, Italian, English, German and, within the foreseeable future, probably also Turkish. Italian, Spanish and Turkish will then be in circulation in Brussels not only as languages of origin of the children of immigrants but also as languages with real European status. This is not unimportant for education. It is an element in the discussion on bicultural educational projects in Brussels that will probably attract ever more attention.

However that may be, Brussels is a city in which divergent linguistic stimuli affect the residents and thus also the children. Multilinguality is here the norm, monolinguality the exception. This is the case already in the indigenous city administration. Whoever speaks about the reception of immigrant children in Dutch-language primary education in Brussels must realise that these children are not being taken up in a monolingual society and not even in a quantitative majority, at least on the local level, but in a quantitative minority.

These three aspects, the increasing European character of Brussels, the general multilinguality, and the minority nature of monolinguality in Dutch, are important determinants for the bicultural educational projects of the Foyer in Brussels.

b. A view of culture and language in immigration

Talking about language education and the knowledge of a language, it should be realised, involves more than just language problems. In fact, the position attributed to a 'language' in education is more than just the selection of a language: it is a cultural option. It is an option that affects the cultural identity of the future adult.

The thesis I would propose is that supporting a subjective cultural identity, which is, after all, a real identity, need not impair the social adjustment of the persons involved or threaten their loyalty to the host country or its inhabitants. The ethnic reference to one's own roots will be more realistic and calm, at least if it does not hinder normal integration into the indigenous society. In Brussels, this is certainly no disadvantage for the reasons sketched above in our view of Brussels society.

At this point, a discussion of the so-called second generation is in order. It is generally accepted that this generation, at least during the school years, seems to be primarily inclined to assimilate the characteristics of the indigenous *Umwelt*, though this inclination is not entirely free of aggression toward the host country. Most often, this becomes apparent as they get a little older. The reason for this is certainly that the children, at a very fragile age, i.e. when they begin school, have seen their authority poles, who represent their language and culture, *de facto* discredited, albeit usually unintentionally, in favour of new authority poles, namely the teachers of the indigenous education system who represent the culture of the host country (see Leman, 1987a: 102–123). It is probably a wise pedagogical measure to give at the very beginning of the school period a very important if not predominant place to teachers who symbolise the culture of origin and who associate as closely as possible with the culture of the immigrant families. Of course, it must be possible to include them in the school curriculum and they must have an open attitude toward the culture of the host country.

c. A view of speaking-thinking and language

To speak a language, to appropriate something in a certain way, implies a judgement of the speaker himself. This thinking and speaking constitute the explicit consciousness, which is simultaneously internal and external. It is this internality that helps constitute the 'self'. The 'self' fully realises itself, becomes 'conscious', only when the prelinguistic level is abandoned for the externality that is proper to every language. Therefore, to recognise oneself 'speaking' in a certain language becomes one of the supports in the development of a child's identity. Frequently there is an interaction between the child's language crisis and its identity crisis.

Very often the language spoken in the immigrant families in Brussels is very fragmentary and 'fluid' in spatial and temporal usage. Sometimes the children, and the second generation, speak another pre-school, first social-isation language than their so-called mother tongue. While one should not neglect the first socialisation language, one also should not isolate, over-emphasise, or situate it outside the broader diachronic and synchronic contexts of immigration. The diachronic context in Brussels implies that at least a number of immigrant languages will become European status languages in the capital of Europe, while in the synchronic context, multilinguality has already become the norm in Brussels, at least for the coming decades.

d. A view of intercultural enrichment

In the realisation of intercultural enrichment, priority is given to the structural over the ideological. Thus, it is important that foreign and native teachers be present on the same level who collaborate closely, that the immigrant children be given the opportunity to explain subject matter elements to the Flemish children and *vice versa*. In other words, there needs to be room for something like experiences that counter the generally prevailing monocultural patterns and that there are built-in opportunities for members of the various subgroups to work together to complete successfully a common task. The intercultural course package must thus provide for real information exchanges between the 'bearers' of cultures under the supervision of co-operating teachers to maintain the level of the exchanges. This must also occur within an operational context in which intergroup contact is actualised on the basis of equality of status without being superficial and without being threatening or competitive.

In summary, the teachers of the culture of origin must be full members of the school team; the teaching materials must be purified of ethnic-specific elements; the children must be able to interact as equal partners; and, most importantly, the school as a whole must be involved in the integration process and must be partially restructured from within on the basis of an internal dynamic.

However, this is easier said than done. For the school is a very complex phenomenon. Here the question arises of innovation strategies in education which of itself can lead again to theoretical considerations which it is not appropriate to discuss here.

Conclusion

The purpose of this chapter has been to review the theoretical basis of the Foyer Model, its historical development in a number of schools, and provide the detailed context for the chapters which follow. These chapters will also be largely concerned with the past and present, with the analysis and evaluation of the Foyer Model as it has so far developed. This is not to say, however, that we are not thinking of the future. It has been pointed out above that the relationship between theory and practice is dynamic, that diachronic change is a feature not only of the Model but also of the Brussels context in which it functions. We shall return, therefore, in the final chapter, to questions and outlook for the future.

References

BYRAM, M. 1987, 'The Foyer Bicultural Education Model: an evaluation'. Durham: internal Foyer report.
DANESI, M. 1987, 'Formal mother-tongue training and the learning of mathematics in elementary school: an observational note on the Brussels Foyer Project'. *Scientia Paedagogica Experimentalis*, 24, 313–320.
FERNÁNDEZ DE ROTA Y MONTER, J.A. and DEL PILAR IRIMIA FERNÁNDEZ, M. 1987, 'Evaluation of the Bicultural Project: The Dutch-Spanish Teaching Encounter at the Foyer Centre in Brussels'. La Coruña: internal Foyer report.
LEMAN, J. 1983, 'Enkele theoretische beschouwingen bij de specificiteit van het bicultureel project van de Foyer te Brussel'. In *Twee Jaar Foyer-Bicultureel te Brussel*. Brussels: Foyer, 48–58.
—— 1985, 'The Foyer Project: A Brussels model of bicultural education in a trilingual situation'. In *Studi Emigrazione — Etudes Migrations*, Rome, 78, 254–266.
—— 1987a, *From Challenging Culture to Challenged Culture*. Leuven: University Press.

—— 1987b, 'Hijos de emigrantes italianos en el proyecto bicultural de una escuela neerlandofona en Bruselas: tres lenguajes, dos culturas y sus interrelaciones'. Paper presented to the symposium 'Lengua y Cultura, aproximación desde una semantica antropologica'. Pazo de Marinan, La Coruña.
LEMMENS, G. and JASPAERT, K. 1987, 'Evaluatie van het Nederlands in het Foyer-bicultureel onderwijsproject'. Tilburg: internal Foyer report.
SPOELDERS, M., LEMAN, J. and SMEEKENS, L. 1985, 'The Brussels Foyer Bicultural Education Project: Socio-cultural background and psycho-educational language assessment'. In G. EXTRA and T. VALLEN (eds), *Ethnic Minorities and Dutch as a Second Language* Dordrecht: Foris, 87–103.

2 Linguistic Evaluation of Dutch as a Third Language

KOEN JASPAERT and GERTRUD LEMMENS

In September 1986, the children with whom the Foyer bicultural programme had started back in 1980, entered the sixth grade of the primary school. They were the first group of children to finish a completely bicultural primary school curriculum. As such they constituted a very interesting group for research: for the first time the overall effects of the Foyer bicultural programme could be evaluated.

It was decided that this evaluation should be carried out by external evaluators. The section Language and Minorities of the Tilburg University was invited to carry out the evaluation of the proficiency in Dutch of these children. This article reports on the evaluation project. In section 1 a general outline of the methodology used will be given. Section 2 contains a description of the tests that were used. In section 3 the main results of the tests will be discussed. In section 4 a further analysis of some of the data will be presented. A number of concluding remarks will be given in section 5.

1. Description of the Evaluation Project

The central question the evaluation project sought to answer was twofold:

—How high is the proficiency in Dutch of children of Italian migrants in Brussels who have been enrolled for six years in the Foyer bicultural programme?

—How does the proficiency in Dutch of the children relate to characteristics of the educational context?

From a methodological point of view, these research questions pose an interesting problem. In general, proficiency could be established along two basic lines. One can either establish measures of language proficiency, or one can try to draw a global impression of proficiency through ethnographic research. In the given research situation, both approaches have serious drawbacks. In order to be able to answer the second research question, and to forward suggestions for the improvement of the educational model on the basis of the results of this study, it is necessary to give a detailed picture of language proficiency. Therefore, it is important not to limit ourselves to the more or less general conclusions that normally emerge from ethnographic studies. We also need to be able to relate that general proficiency to certain important sub-proficiencies. On the other hand, the group of children to be investigated is too small to allow the results of language tests to be related to characteristics of the model with a certain degree of confidence. Individual characteristics of the children may influence the results to a great extent, thus blurring the effect of didactic choices made in the model.

This dilemma could not be solved. The only thing we could do was try to find ways to minimalise its effects. We opted for a research design in which ample attention was given to ethnographic research as well as to the establishment of language measures.

The ethnographic research focused on the school setting within which the children acquired Dutch. Through participatory observation some aspects of the language learning process were investigated: quality and quantity of the language input, effectiveness of the communication, children's opportunities to use and practise Dutch (cf. Fillmore, 1982; Rivers, 1976). In addition more objective data on the educational setting were collected through structured observations. The observation scheme used for these observations concentrated on the interaction between teacher and pupil. The analysis of this interaction is essential to an understanding of the classroom situation in which the pupils have to function (Mehan, 1985; Green & Wallat, 1981). Moreover, the use of structured observations made a comparison between classes easier.

In this article we shall concentrate on the quantitative analysis of the language tests used in the evaluation project. The outcomes of the more qualitative analysis based on the observations is discussed elsewhere (Lemmens & Jaspaert, 1987).

For the establishment of language proficiency measures, we made use of language tests. We tried to reduce the negative effect of the small size of the experimental group in two ways. We administered a large number of very different language tests, and we incorporated in the research design a large number of control groups. Both approaches were aimed at reducing the danger of erroneously attributing certain characteristics of the language proficiency within the experimental group to choices made in the educational model. By enlarging the diversity of tests, testing procedures and testing moments, we hope to have reduced the influence on the overall test result of idiosyncratic factors such as fatigue, aversion towards certain tests or test procedures and so on. Through the introduction of a large number of control groups we want to be able to abstract as much as possible from individual traits of pupils in the experimental group.

The selection of tests and control groups was complicated by the peculiar language situation of the children in the experimental group. As is described elsewhere in this volume, Dutch should be regarded as a third language for the Italian children in the Brussels area. In most cases their home language is Italian or a dialect of Italian, whereas French is the language dominating the world outside the home and the school. The peculiarity of this situation has its effects on the comparability of the Brussels situation with other parts of the Dutch language area. One cannot expect the children of the experimental group to perform as well on Dutch proficiency tests as children for whom Dutch is a genuine second language. Nevertheless, we are forced to work with tests that have been developed for children in The Netherlands or Flanders. It is also very difficult to find suitable control groups in the Brussels area: most children of Italian origin in Brussels who are not enrolled in a bicultural project go to French schools. So we also selected a number of control groups outside Brussels.

Another factor complicating the choice of tests is that most tests, constructed for the measurement of proficiency in Dutch, have been developed in The Netherlands, and do not take into account the variation in the Dutch standard language. Within the Dutch standard language two basic varieties can be distinguished. Recent sociolinguistic research (Deprez, 1982; Jaspaert, 1986) has shown that a Flemish variety of Dutch has emerged. The question as to how different this variety is from the standard Dutch of The Netherlands has not been answered adequately. It seems safe to assume, however, that the standard language with which the children in the Brussels Foyer schools are confronted differs considerably from the standard language contacts of children in Dutch schools. This difference is stressed by differences in language background of the teachers (Flemish teachers have a dialect background more often than their Dutch counterparts). Moreover, Dutch children are in general considered more 'fluent' in Dutch than Flemish children, a fact that can probably be related to differences in the didactic approach to language teaching.

A further consideration that influenced our choice of language tests is that the experimental group in this study had been tested on numerous occasions in the past. The reapplication of the tests that were used in these studies would therefore have the advantage of providing longitudinal data on the progress children make. Moreover, by selecting as a control group the children that are enrolled in the same classes as the experimental group at the moment of the former administration of the tests, information on the generalisability of the test results can be obtained, and, in this way, part of the problem of working with a small experimental group can be overcome. A serious disadvantage connected with the use of these tests, however, is that in most cases they are meant to be used with younger children. We have chosen to use some of these tests, in particular those that yielded low scores on earlier test occasions. One should keep in mind that the fact that these tests were really intended for younger children may have an effect on the results.

The tests were given to children in five schools. Not all children took every test. Since the tests that were administered to the children in school five are not discussed here, we shall not describe this group of informants. School one is the school in which the bicultural project originally started. All Italian children in this school follow the bicultural education programme. In school two the bicultural programme started two years later. This means that the Italian children in class six of this school have followed the same curriculum as the Belgian children throughout the primary school. School three has a bicultural project involving Spanish children. Here the oldest biculturally educated children were in class five at the moment this study was carried out. School four is a secondary school in the province of Limburg, in which a lot of children of Italian origin are enrolled. These children were included in the research design as a control group in order to be able to get an idea of how elaborate proficiency in Dutch needs to be for successful participation in secondary education.

Together with the description of each test in section 2, the sample for that particular test will be given.

2. Description of Tests

2.1 Language proficiency test developed in Utrecht (UTANT)

The UTANT was intended as an instrument for the measurement of the language proficiency of four- to six-year-old children with low social background. Three of its four subtests are based on the Illinois Test of Psycholinguistic Abilities (ITPA). Since the fourth subtest turned out to be unreliable (Kohnstamm, 1983: 57), we administered only the subtests:

A: Passive vocabulary (35 items)
B: Analogies and contrasts (25 items)
C: Morphological rules (20 items).

Table 1 shows to which groups this test was administered.

TABLE 1 *Survey of Administration History of UTANT*

Class	1	2	3	4	5	6
School 1						
Moment of admin.						
Dec. 1982		$X + C_B$				
June 1983		X				
Nov. 1983			$X + C_B$			
June 1984			X			
Jan. 1987	C_I	C	C_I		C_I	$X + C_B$
School 2						
Jan. 1987	C_I	C_I				C_I

X = experimental group
C_I, C_B = control group of Italian/Belgian children
C = control group with Italian children and control groups with Belgian children

2.2 Grammatical Analysis Test (GAT)

The GAT is a test that aims at providing a detailed and reliable diagnosis of the grammatical competence of children between four and seven years old (Van Geert, 1977). It is based on the principle that linguistic input can be selected in such a way that subjects need a thorough knowledge of the grammatical structures involved in order to reach an adequate semantic analysis of the sentence that is presented to them.

In the test, subjects are asked to combine Dutch syntactic structures with one of a series of drawings. The test contains 50 such items.

The administration history of the test resembles that of the UTANT closely (cf. Table 1). In 1987 the test was also administered to the Belgian students in class three and the Italian and Belgian students in class four of the first school, whereas class five of school one and class one of school two did not participate.

2.3 One-minute test (BRUS)

The BRUS is a test of technical reading proficiency aimed at children from the second to the sixth class of the primary school. It consists of a list of 116 unrelated words, ordered in ascending reading difficulty. Subjects are asked to read the words fast and clearly. The score on the test represents the number of words that were correctly read within one minute. The sample for this test is given in Table 2.

TABLE 2 *Survey of Administration History of BRUS*

Class	1	2	3	4	5	6
School 1						
Moment of admin.						
Nov. 1984				$X+C_B$		
June 1985				X		
Jan. 1987		C		C	C	$X+C_B$
School 2						
Jan. 1987		C				C_I

2.4 Test for pupils with mother tongue other than Dutch (IA)

The IA is developed as a means to establish the level of proficiency in Dutch of children with a non-Dutch linguistic background. It has as its main purpose the enabling of the adaptation of education to the proficiency level of these children. The test consists of a number of subtests, split up in different levels. The lowest level corresponds to a near absence of proficiency in Dutch. The highest level (level three) indicates that instruction in Dutch can be followed.

By means of the IA, reading and writing proficiency was tested. For reading, two different subtests were administered. In each of these tests subjects were asked to answer a number of multiple choice questions concerning a story they had just read. For writing, three different assignments were given (filling out of a form, completing a letter to a friend and writing a column for the school paper).

The test was originally meant for children from 12 to 16 years old. Prior application has made clear, however, that it can also be used with children from 9 to 12.

The test was, prior to our research, administered to the experimental group and their Belgian classmates in November 1984, and to the experimental group alone some months later. In 1987 the test was administered in the fourth and the sixth class (I + B) of school one.

In school two only the Italian children of the sixth class took part.

2.5 Dictation

The dictation that was used in this study consisted of nine separate sentences and a number of unrelated words. It should not be considered a pragmatic test (Van Els *et al.*, 1984; Oller, 1979), but merely a spelling test. The test was administered to the same groups as the IA (cf. 2.4).

2.6 Reading comprehension (versions one and two)

As a reading comprehension test, subjects are given written instructions for the execution of 30 tasks. These tasks are kept very simple, so that the inability to carry them out can be attributed to a deficient comprehension of the instructions (Brus & Van Bergen, 1972). The instructions are ordered in ascending difficulty. The test is meant for pupils in the second to the fourth class. The first version of the test was administered to the same groups that took the IA and the dictation. In addition, a second version of the test was administered to all pupils in the sixth class in school one and to the Italian pupils in the sixth class in school two.

2.7 Cloze and editing test

In addition to the test directly measuring some aspects of language proficiency, we also included two global proficiency tests. The cloze test that was used was drawn from the research project on the relation between Dutch as a second language and achievement at the end of primary school, that is currently being carried out by Kerkhoff (Kerkhoff & Vallen, 1984). It is a fixed ratio test, in which every seventh word has been dropped. The editing test is part of the IA. Neither of the tests has previously been administered to children in the Foyer project. Since no longitudinal comparison of results was possible, we enlarged the sample for these tests by including two new control groups. One of these groups comes from a Brussels primary school that houses a bicultural programme for Spanish children (school three). The oldest children in that programme have reached the fifth class. These children, together with the Belgian children in their class, were asked to take both the cloze and the editing test. The other group consists of Italian students in the first year of a secondary school in Limburg (school four). By including the Spanish children, we tried to move away a little bit from the possible idiosyncrasy of the experimental group, and check whether some more general characteristics of the language proficiency of children in the Foyer model could be found. The Limburg group was expected to provide an idea of how proficient a subject needed to be in order to be able to follow secondary education in Dutch. Of course, it would have been much better to find a control group for this purpose in the Brussels neighbourhood, but, unfortunately, no Dutch-language secondary school in Brussels had sufficient students of Italian origin (or, in fact, of any origin other than Belgian) enrolled.

Apart from these two groups, these tests were taken by all pupils in the sixth classes of schools one and two. For the cloze test an exact scoring procedure was followed, not taking into account spelling errors. The editing test was corrected disregarding the words that were erroneously struck out. Maximum scores were respectively 59 and 49.

3. Results

3.1 UTANT

As a first step in the analysis of the UTANT data, we have checked whether the longitudinal data differed significantly from the cross-sectional data and whether the factor 'school' had a significant effect on the test results. The only effect along these lines that could be established is the influence of the type of data on the scores for subtest B: the experimental group scored considerably higher when they were in second grade than the children who attended the second class in 1987. So, except for this one effect, we do not have to take into account the school where, and the moment of measurement when, the data were collected. The scores on the subtest A show no significant difference between Belgian and Italian children. From class two onward, the scores of both groups tend towards the maximum. When the extremely low scores of the children that were in class two in 1987 are disregarded, subtest B offers more or less the same picture: no significant difference between Belgians and Italians, and a tendency towards maximum scores from the third class onward. Both tests turn out to be too easy for the group under investigation. The only thing that can be inferred from them is that the children from the experimental group possess at least the basic skills necessary for these tests.

Only subtest C shows a significant effect of the factor 'nationality' ($F = 6.31$; $p = 0.014$; analysis of variance with class and nationality as independent variables). The Italian children score systematically lower than the Belgian children. A slight ceiling effect can be detected in the scores of the Belgian children in class six (cf. Table 3).

TABLE 3 *Mean Scores for Three Subtests of UTANT; Cross-Sectional and Longitudinal Data*

Class		1	2	3	5	6
Group						
Italians	A	20	25.8	29.2	30.6	31.5
	B	9.2	13.6	18.2	17	21.8
	C	2.1	5.7	9.5	10.4	14.9
	n	10	36	24	5	8
Belgians	A	—	28.3	33.0	31.7	31.5
	B	—	14.0	21.0	22.8	21.6
	C	—	6.7	12.5	16.0	16.5
	n		15	2	6	6

3.2 GAT

The means, standard deviations and number of subjects of the cross-sectional data from the children of school one are presented in Table 4.

The results suggest that skills in grammatical analysis develop more slowly in the Italian group, but that, by the end of the primary school, both groups reach a comparable level of skill. The experimental group, i.e. the Italian children of the sixth class, even score slightly higher than their Belgian counterparts.

TABLE 4 *Mean Scores, Standard Deviations for Classes and Nationality Groups on GAT*

Class		1	2	3	4	6
Group						
Italians	X	22.2	25.8	27.7	31.9	41.7
	N	5	6	6	7	6
	s	6.87	4.49	6.68	3.53	3.32
Belgians	X	—	31.9	32.8	39.7	39.5
	N		8	6	3	6
	s		5.82	3.25	3.5	6.02

When the longitudinal data are also taken into account, the slower development in Italian children becomes less clear. The experimental group scored an average 30.5 (s = 2.95) in class two and 34.7 (s = 4.37) in class three. These scores are considerably higher than the scores of the children in class two and class three in the cross-sectional data. The Belgian children of class six reached an average score of 36 (s = 7.32) at the 1984 measuring moment, when they attended class three. This score is higher than the score of the Belgian children in class three in the cross-sectional data, but is hardly better than the score of the experimental group at the same measuring moment. So it seems that the low scores of the Italian children in class three (and, to a lesser extent, two and four) in the cross-sectional data do not necessarily point towards a slower development of grammatical analysis skills in the Italian children. The large standard deviation, mainly due to the extremely low scores of two of the children in this group, suggests that idiosyncratic characteristics within the group may have caused the impression of slower development.

A comparison of the results from the two schools in which this test was administered yields no significant differences. The Italian children in the second class of school two average 27.2 on the test (N = 6; s = 4.06). The two Italian sixth-graders in this school score slightly lower than the average score of the comparable group in school one. It is interesting to note that these two children, who have not been enrolled in bicultural education, score on most other tests comparable to the best subjects in the experimental group.

These results seem to point out that the grammatical analysis skills of the children from the bicultural education programme, and more specifically of those of the experimental group, are better than can be expected on the basis of their general language proficiency skills. We will come back to this later.

3.3 BRUS

The figures in Table 5 give a rough indication of the reading proficiency of the subjects. In school one, the Italian children score systematically lower than the Belgian children. The gap between the two groups narrows as the children become older. One could wonder whether the narrowing gap has anything to do with the Belgian children approaching some limit. The average score does not improve between classes five and six. A comparable evolution is seen when the longitudinal data are taken into account. The experimental group scored 40.17 when they were in class four, their Belgian counterparts averaged 55 at that time. So, whereas the scores of the Italian children improved considerably, those of the Belgian subjects improved only slightly.

An important question in interpreting the gap between the scores of Belgian and Italian subjects is whether the relatively low score of the Italian

TABLE 5 *Mean Scores, Standard Deviations and Cell Frequency for BRUS, Cross-Sectional Data*

		School 1				School 2	
		2	4	5	6	2	6
Italians	X	12.17	32	42	47.6	23.5	78
	n	6	7	5	6	6	2
	s	5.71	12.69	8.8	14.26	4.59	1
Belgians	X	24.75	48	59.16	58.66	19.2	—
	n	8	3	6	6	5	
	s	9.08	4.58	16.75	7.06	5.08	

children is an indication of a slower reading speed or of the fact that they make a lot of errors. Since the number of incorrectly read words was not registered, it is impossible at this stage to answer this question. A discussion of the scores on the BRUS in connection with the scores on other tests (cf. section 4) might clarify the matter. However, from the notes that were taken during the administration of the test it could be inferred that no mistakes occur that are typical for the Italian group. This observation suggests that the Italian children do not really lag behind in technical reading skills: they either read more slowly, or they make the same mistakes more frequently than the Belgian children. In both instances, their arrears have more to do with proficiency and practice than with technical skill.

3.4 IA

3.4.1 Writing tests

As was indicated in section 2.4, three writing tests were used. In the first of these tests subjects were asked to fill out a form. All children from the sixth class managed to provide the information asked for. Just as in the case of the first part of the UTANT (cf. section 3.1) we can only conclude that the test does not discriminate for our experimental group. Whereas both the cross-sectional and the longitudinal data point out that most children in class four do not possess the necessary skills to carry out the task with complete adequacy ($X = 11.25$), by the time they are in the sixth class they have acquired that skill ($X = 14.17$). This holds for the Italian as well as for the Belgian children, although we need to point out here that we did not have any longitudinal data on the Belgian children that were in class six at the moment of this study.

In subtest 2 children were asked to add to a letter written to a friend. The test was scored in two ways. A first score only represents the adequacy of the information given. For the second score spelling and grammar of what was filled in was taken into account also (cf. Table 6). The first score yields more or less the same picture as the first subtest. The children in class four are not able yet to provide adequate information in all instances (X = 13.66), whereas most children in class six manage to do so on most occasions (X = 14.5). The average for the children in class six is kept relatively low by the exceptionally low score of two Belgian children (10 and 11).

TABLE 6 *IA, Writing Subtest 2: Average scores for formally correct and adequate information, cross-sectional data*

		School 1		School 2
		4	*6*	*6*
Belgians	X	14.5/12.5	13.5/11.5	—
	n	2	6	
Italians	X	13.3/6	15/9.33	15.5/13
	n	7	6	2

The second score shows a lot more variation.

For all groups, there is a discrepancy between the adequacy of the information and the correctness of the form in which it is given. This discrepancy is much larger for the Italian children in school one than for the Belgian children, and larger for the Italian children in class four than for those in class six. From these results a number of conclusions can be drawn. The comprehension skill of the Italian children in both class four and class six seems developed enough to understand and adequately respond to the task presented to them. Their productive writing skills, however, lag behind. As we have seen in other tests, part of the arrears have been overcome by the time the children are in class six, but there still is an important difference between the discrepancy between both scores of the Italian and those of the Belgian children. The longitudinal data corroborate this result. At an earlier moment of measurement, when the experimental group attended class four, they scored an average of 13.5 for score one (with one child scoring as low as 7) and 7.66 for score two. From a qualitative analysis of the scores, it turns out that the low scores on linguistic correctness in class six are not due to mistakes with the more technical aspects of the writing process, such as spelling, but rather to mistakes such as wrong word order and use of tenses. In class four this is much more the case. It should also be noted that the children in class six give much more elaborate information. This does not improve their scores; on the contrary, since they are using more 'language', they run a greater risk of making errors. This explains why the linguistic correctness score of the children in the sixth class is not all that much higher than that of the children in class four, although they make comparatively fewer technical writing errors.

Another interesting aspect of the scores in Table 6 is that the Italian subjects in school two do not show the same discrepancy between informational adequacy and linguistic correctness. They, too, took the same test when they attended class four. These data show no discrepancy, either ($X = 15.66/ 14.66$; $N = 3$). Although we have to be very careful not to attach too much importance to these scores, since the number of subjects is very low, these results seem to suggest that the observed discrepancy in the scores of the Italian group in school one has something to do with the bicultural model. In most tests we have observed that the Italian children in school two obtained results comparable to those of the best children in school one. For this test, or rather for subscore 2, they actually do better.

The third writing subtest of the IA, a short composition, shows more or less the same picture as the first one. The test was scored by attributing to each text a level of adequacy (A, B or C, C being the highest level). In establishing levels of adequacy, elements such as coherence and accuracy of description are taken into account, together with linguistic correctness. In class four all children are classified in level A. All Belgian children of class six, except for one, end up in level B. Of the Italian children of class six, three reached C, two B and one A. Of the two Italian children from the sixth class in school two, one got C and the other one B. Longitudinal comparison for this test is not interesting, since the scoring of this test differs for each moment of measurement. So, again, the experimental group performs well, even better than their Belgian classmates, and at least as well as the Italian children in school two. They also do much better than the children, both Belgian and Italian, of class four.

3.4.2 Subtest comprehensive reading

From Table 7 it can be inferred that the reliability of test 1 (maximum score = 15) is rather doubtful. A ceiling effect occurs for the Belgian children in class four and for the Italian children in class six. The Belgian children in class six, however, have a comparatively low score. In view of the scores of the other groups, it is improbable that this low score represents the true proficiency level of the Belgian children of class six. The fact that in the second test, which is supposed to measure a higher level of comprehensive skill, shows an opposite relation supports this interpretation.

TABLE 7 *Average Scores on Reading Subtests of IA*

		School 1		School 2
		4	*6*	*6*
Belgians	test 1	13.6	11.7	—
	test 2	10.3	14.5	
Italians	test 1	10.3	13	13
	test 2	10.3	13	16

The second test yields more interesting results. All group scores are quite some way removed from the maximum score of 20. The Italian children in class four do equally well as their Belgian classmates. Both groups in class six score better than the groups in class four. Whereas for most tests which show improvement for both Italians and Belgians, the improvement of the Italian is usually higher than that of the Belgian children, for this test it is clearly the Belgian group which shows the larger improvement. At this point in the discussion, this result can still be interpreted in many ways. Since a number of comprehensive reading tests still need to be discussed, we shall not go into these interpretations here. We shall pay ample attention to comprehensive reading in the general discussion of the test results (section 4).

3.5 Dictation

The dictation resulted in three separate scores, the third of which relates to spelling mistakes in the list of unrelated words. The first score represents the number of words that were mis-spelled in the nine sentences that constituted the first part of the dictation. The second score relates to the number of 'other errors' in these sentences: punctuation, hyphenation, omission of words and the like.

For both the Belgian and Italian groups, the children from class six perform clearly better than the children from class four. In class four, the Italian children score considerably worse than their Belgian classmates. In class six, the gap between the two groups has been narrowed down for the greater part. In fact, when one looks at the individual score, one notices that the difference in scores between these groups is entirely due to the extremely low score of one of the children (26/5/6). The averages for the three scores without this subject are 2.8, 1.8 and 2.4. So only for the list of unrelated words can the scores of the Italian group be said to be higher.

TABLE 8 *Average Scores on Dictation, Cross-Sectional Data*

		School 1 4	School 1 6	School 2 6
Belgians	s 1	7	2.17	—
	s 2	2.66	1.67	
	s 3	5	0.83	
	n	3	6	
Italians	s 1	17	6.67	0.5
	s 2	4.14	2.33	1
	s 3	5.71	3	0.5
	n	7	6	2

The longitudinal data yield a comparable picture. When the experimental group attended class four, they obtained the following average scores (without the extremely low-scoring subject, who was absent when the test was administered): 10.4/3.6/5.8.

The Italian children from school two do very well on the dictation. One of them is even the only subject of the whole sample who does not make any mistake at all. The improvement they make in comparison to the scores they obtained when they were in class four, is much less spectacular than for the experimental group (4.66/0.66/3.33: N = 3).

So, again we see that the children enrolled in the bicultural education programme score worse than their Belgian classmates in class four, but that by the time they are in class six, the arrears have disappeared.

As to the qualitative analysis of the spelling mistakes, we shall limit ourselves here to the observation that, in accordance with what was found in other research, the Italian children do not seem to make typical mistakes. If they spell less well, they make the same mistakes as the Belgian children, but make them more often (cf. Oller, 1979).

3.6 Comprehensive reading

In Table 9 the results on both versions of the comprehensive reading test are presented.

The longitudinal data for the experimental group compare very well with the score of the Italian group of class four in the cross-sectional data (X = 15.7). So, as was the case for most previous tests, the Italian group scores considerably lower than the Belgian group in class four. Part of the gap between the two groups has disappeared in class six (although one has to be careful with this observation, considering the small number of subjects, particularly in the Belgian group in class four). Still the difference between these groups in class six is larger than what was found for most other tests, especially with regard to test two.

TABLE 9 *Average Scores on Comprehensive Reading Tests, Cross-Sectional Data*

| | | School 1 | | School 2 |
		4	6	6
Belgians				
test 1	X	20	24.2	—
test 2	X	—	18.8	
	n	3	6	
Italians				
test 1	X	14.7	21.7	25.5
test 2	X	—	13.5	19
	n	7	6	2

As was the case with the dictation, the average scores are influenced by the very low scores of one of the Italian subjects of class six (16 on test one; 3 on test two). The averages without this subject amount to 22.8 on test one and 15.6 on test two. But in the Belgian group, too, there are two subjects who performed badly on these tests, so that even without the low-scoring subject, the Italian group does not really attain the level of the Belgian group.

The two Italian children from school two score even better than the Belgian children in class six of school one. So, here, too, the difference in scores between the Italian children that are enrolled in the bicultural project and the children that are not is slightly larger than with most other tests.

So, once again it seems that comprehensive reading might be a skill that is distributed differently from other skills with regard to children enrolled in the bicultural curriculum (cf. section 3.4.2). It is, of course, true that the differences that were observed here only give a slight indication in that direction, and that, in view of the limitations of the sample, extreme care is warranted. Therefore, we shall come back to this issue in the last section, in which the information of all tests is brought together.

3.7 Cloze and editing test

Table 10 gives an overview of the average scores on both tests. The sample to which these tests were administered was rather different from that for the other tests (for a description, cf. section 2.7).

TABLE 10 *Mean Scores on Cloze and Editing Test*

	CLOZE	EDIT	n
School one			
Italians	12.3	28.8	6
Belgians	18.3	35.3	6
School two	24.7	43	8
School three			
Spanish	15	34	4
Belgians	21.2	38.5	23
School four			
A	19.2	43.4	12
B	15.9	38.5	7

The maximal score on the cloze test and editing test is respectively 59 and 49. The overall average score for both tests is 19.2 and 39.6 These figures illustrate an important difference between the two tests. The editing test turned out to be relatively easy, whereas the cloze test was really difficult. Nevertheless, the correlation between the two tests is relatively high ($r = 0.64$; $p \leq 0.001$). Since both tests were meant as general measures of proficiency, the occurrence of the correlation is not surprising.

We regard the level of difficulty of the editing test as corresponding rather well with the level of proficiency that is needed to make a successful transition from the primary to the secondary school. In other words children who are sufficiently proficient in Dutch to move on to secondary education are expected to do very well on this test. This assumption is based on the average scores of the different groups. As can be observed in Table 10 children in school four, for instance (especially those in class A), do very well in the test. These children have already finished primary school. The subjects in class A, in particular, have been judged to have sufficient proficiency in Dutch to follow regular secondary school courses. The scores of the children in school three are a bit lower, but that, too, is logical since these children attend class five of primary school, and, consequently, have another year to attain the level of proficiency necessary to move on to secondary school.

On the whole there are only two scores which need further investigation: both the experimental group and their Belgian classmates score unexpectedly low on the editing test. In both cases the low average score has been caused by two children with an exceptionally low individual score (9 for two Italian children, 15 and 25 for the two Belgian children). One Italian child scores around the group average, the three others all score 40 or more. So these scores suggest that at least three out of the six Italian children have acquired a sufficient overall proficiency in Dutch to move on to secondary education. For the Belgian children in class six of school one, the results confirm the impression of rather low proficiency that already emerged from the results on the other tests.

The scores on the cloze test yield more or less the same picture as the scores on the edit test. Again, the Belgian children from school one score rather low in comparison to the Belgian children in school two and school three (which are, in fact, one year younger). The individual scores of the children in the experimental group are also comparable to their editing scores. The most important difference between the scores on the cloze and the editing test is that the general score of the Belgian children on the cloze test is clearly higher than the score of the Italian and Spanish children. This has to do with the level of difficulty of the test: whereas the editing test did not discriminate between sufficient and more than sufficient levels of proficiency with regard to the transition to secondary school (assuming that our interpretation of the level of difficulty of the edit test is correct), the cloze test does. So, the difference in score pattern between the two tests does not necessitate altering the interpretation of the editing scores. The cloze scores indicate that the conclusions about a number of the Italian children reaching a sufficient level of proficiency does not imply that they have caught up completely with the Belgian children of their age.

4. Some Further Analyses

Although it is very difficult to compare results of different bicultural programmes to each other, and the peculiarity of the Brussels setting makes comparison even more risky, the positive result of the children in the Foyer project seems to corroborate what Appel and Muysken (1987) see as a general trend in studies on bilingual programmes: the ample attention given to the first language does not hamper seriously the acquisition of a second (or, in this case, a third) language.

In general the picture that emerged from the discussion of the tests in the previous section is that children in the experimental group succeed in catching up on most of their arrears in proficiency in the course of primary school. The test results also indicated that the degree of success varies with regard to different elements of this general proficiency and to individual children.

In section 3 the analysis of the results concentrated on group scores on individual tests. This procedure left a number of questions concerning the variation within the experimental group and between separate aspects of proficiency unanswered. We did point out a number of times that a given group score was influenced negatively by extremely low scores of some children. Such a low score may be incidental, a result of idiosyncratic factors which cause a child to perform badly on one test or at one moment, or it may be the result of a deviant proficiency of that child with regard to one or more specific aspects of proficiency. We have also pointed out a number of times that although most tests (except for the editing and cloze tests) are designed to measure some specific aspects of language proficiency, other proficiency elements interfered from time to time, influencing the test score.

In order to get some insight into the relationship between tests and the individual proficiency structure of each subject, a re-analysis of the test results was necessary. For this purpose a factor analysis was carried out in which all but three test scores were entered of the 14 children that had taken all the tests. This group of 14 children consisted of all children of class six in school one and the two Italian children of class six in school two. It should be noted that this limited sample does not allow for cross-sectional or longitudinal comparison of subjects of different age groups.

The writing tests 1 and 3 and the reading test 1 of the IA were not entered in the factor analysis. Writing 1 and reading 1 turned out to be too easy for the children of class six, so that the scores on these tests show hardly any variance.

TABLE 11 *Rotated Factor Matrix*

	factor 1	factor 2
UTANT A	0.89	0.26
UTANT B	0.85	0.27
UTANT C	0.12	0.89
GAT	0.94	-0.16
BRUS	0.24	0.70
Dictation score 1	-0.22	-0.86
Dictation score 2	-0.29	-0.79
Dictation score 3	-0.03	-0.92
IA writing 2/score 1	0.84	0.12
IA writing 2/score 2	0.54	0.63
IA reading 2	0.68	0.46
Comp. reading 1	0.73	0.61
Comp. reading 2	0.77	0.57
Edit	0.68	0.53
Cloze	0.61	0.58

Writing 3 was scored in a more qualitative way, so that its intepretation in quantitative terms becomes complicated.

Fourteen different scores were entered in the factor analysis. It resulted in a very good two-factorial solution (explained variance = 77.3%), in which factor 1 is clearly much more important than factor 2 (eigenvalues of 9.18 and 2.42). The rotated factor matrix is presented in Table 11.

On the basis of the factor loadings in Table 11, the tests can be divided into three groups. UTANT A and B, GAT and IA writing 2/score 1 load high on factor 1 and low on factor 2; the three dictation scores, BRUS and UTANT C load high on factor 2 and low on factor 1; all other tests load to an important extent on both factors. On the basis of this division an interpretation of the two factors can be proposed. The second group, loading high on factor 2, contains tests in which what we would like to call 'technical aspects' of language proficiency hold a central position: spelling, technical reading and morphological knowledge (very often about exceptions to more general rules). Most tests scoring high on factor 1 draw heavily on more comprehensive skills. The scores in the third group are then related to both technical and comprehensive skills. A nice example of this division is formed by the two scores on the test IA writing 2. The first score, representing the adequacy of the information given, belongs in the first group. The second score, for which the linguistic correctness of the information has also been taken into account, loads relatively high on both dimensions.

The only problem for this interpretation is formed by the three tests on comprehensive reading (comp. reading 1 and 2 and IA reading 2). Contrary to what one would expect on the basis of the interpretation of the factor analysis, these tests do not belong to group one (factor 1) but to group three (both factors). The position of these tests seems to suggest that the interpretation in terms of technical versus comprehensive skills only gives part of the picture.

In the discussion of the tests loading high on factor 2 in section 3, it has been observed a number of times that for these tests the children in the experimental group performed slightly worse than their Belgian classmates, and that this was not the case for the tests loading on factor 1. This observation suggests an alternative interpretation for the two factors that resulted from the analysis. In this interpretation factor 1 represents systematic variation in test scores which is not related to differences between the experimental group and the control group, and factor 2 represents variation in scores for which this is systematically the case. As a check on this interpretation and, at the same time, as an illustration, we have plotted the factor scores of all subjects on both factors (Figure 1).

It is clear from Figure 1 that the children of the experimental group do not score differently from the control group children on factor 1, but score systematically lower on factor 2. It is important here to remember that the variation represented by factor 1 is much more important than the variation represented in factor 2. This means that in class six there are more important divisions between pupils to be made than between Italian and Belgian children.

As Figure 1 shows, there is really only one Italian child that scores drastically lower on factor 2 than the rest of the group. For the other children, the difference in score with the Belgian children is minimal.

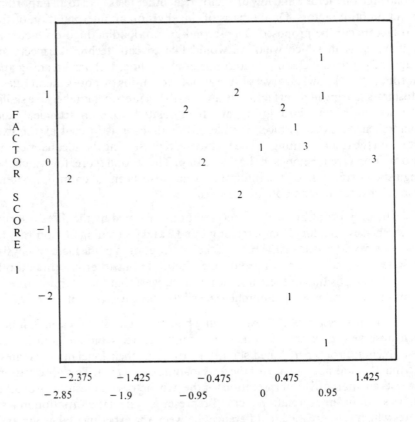

FACTOR SCORE 2

FIGURE 1 *Plot of Factor Scores*
         1 = School 1, class 6, Belgian children
         2 = School 1, class 6, Italian children
         3 = School 2, class 6, Italian children

Another interesting point that can be inferred from Figure 1 is that the Italian children from school two score higher than the experimental group on factor 2 but not on factor 1. So factor 2 represents a difference between Italian children in the bicultural programme and the others rather than a difference between Italian and Belgian children. The interpretation of the two factors in terms of group rather than test characteristics does not do away with the fact that certain tests are typical of one or the other factor. So the question of the interpretation of the factors in terms of tests, or rather in terms of the language proficiency skills the tests are supposed to have measured, needs to be considered again.

Group 1 (tests loading high on factor 1) consists of tests on which both the experimental group and the control group get an average score that is relatively close to the maximum. Within the groups, however, there is some degree of variation: a number of children in both groups actually do get a maximum score, whereas some others may score considerably lower. It is an important merit of the factor analysis that it shows that the ceiling effect that was observed for some groups and some tests actually hides a considerable amount of systematic variation within the groups. In this manner tests that did not seem to yield interesting information, turn out to contain interpretable results.

Figure 1 shows that two Belgian children in particular score systematically rather low. All the tests in the first group measure to some extent a form of comprehension. As was pointed out earlier, comprehension, together with more technical skills, loads high on factor 2 as well. The comprehension that is measured by the tests loading on factor 2, however, differs from the elements of comprehension that are contained in factor 1. In relation to factor 1 comprehension stands for passive semantic knowledge of individual linguistic elements. The comprehension element in factor 2 is much more integral in nature. Whereas the tests in group one concentrate on, for instance, passive vocabulary (UTANT A) or understanding of grammatical structures (GAT), the tests loading on factor 2 that deal with comprehension require the understanding of larger parts of texts, stories or verbal tasks. This second form of comprehension includes not only the comprehension of the separate elements that constitute the text, but also requires the ability to combine these elements into meaningful sequences. So, with relation to comprehension we suggest that the factorial structure should be interpreted as evidence of the fact that the children in the experimental group comprehend individual linguistic elements of Dutch we have tested as well as the children in the control group, but have more difficulties in applying this knowledge to the comprehension of more elaborate linguistic products. This does not mean, of course, that the analysis shows that both groups have equal knowledge of separate linguistic elements. In view of the high group scores on the tests in group one, it may very well be the case that there is still a difference in this form of comprehension for which the tests that were used did not discriminate. The important point here is that the correlation between the comprehension dimensions we have distinguished is different for the two groups: the Italian children turn out to have more difficulty in applying their comprehension of separate linguistic elements to the more integral comprehension of language.

To a greater extent than by integral comprehension, factor 2 is characterised by high loadings of tests measuring more technical skills. At first sight, this seems to be a contradiction: these technical skills consist of separate elements of knowledge that relate intuitively better to comprehension of separate elements than to what we called integral comprehension. Knowing a spelling rule is much more like knowing the meaning of a word than like having an understanding of the flow of a story. On closer examination, however, the position of these technical skills in the factor solution turns out to be quite logical. First of all, the tests measured productive skills: the reproduction of rules was not asked, but their application in context. In this sense these tests differ drastically from the tests that are typical of factor 1. Moreover, we have pointed out in section 3 that the lower score of children in the experimental group on some of the 'technical' tests did not seem caused by the fact that they made certain types of mistakes the other children did not make. All children made the same mistakes, but the children in the experimental group made them more often than the other children. This could be interpreted in the sense that their knowledge of the technical rules is comparable to that of the other children, but that they have more difficulty applying these rules to larger productive tasks. This interpretation corresponds very well with the interpretation in terms of comprehension that was given to the two factors earlier.

The fact that the editing and cloze tests load on both factors fits nicely with the interpretation of these factors that has been proposed. In order to do well on these tests, one needs an understanding of separate linguistic elements (e.g. words to be struck out or filled in) as well as an understanding of the text. These two tests can be called general in the sense that they measure both factors that have been observed in the proficiency of the children at the same time.

The only test loading that is counter-indicative to the factor interpretation so far is the high loading of UTANT C on factor 2. In this test morphological knowledge was measured in a non-integrated way. There is a significant difference between the scores of Italian and Belgian children on this test (section 3.1). This test confirms that there still is a difference in knowledge of separate linguistic elements between the two groups. As was pointed out, the other tests did not allow for definite conclusions regarding this issue. But here, too, the difference that occurs is rather slight. One should also remember that in this factor analysis no data on other age groups have been included. The discussion of the evolution in scores with age in section 3 has made clear that the Italian children that are enrolled in the bicultural model rapidly close the initial gap between their knowledge of separate linguistic elements and that of their classmates. The factor analysis shows that by the time they have reached class six, some differences between the two groups still exist (in morphology, and possibly also in some other areas), but that these do not constitute a serious problem.

An analysis of the items of the UTANT C shows that the difference in scores between the experimental and the control group is entirely due to items that represent morphological irregularities. The process of vowel change in the root word that occurs in a number of unproductive flectional word formation processes in Dutch causes a serious problem for the experimental group.

5. Conclusions

In spite of the many *caveats* that needed to be formulated at the outset of this article regarding the use of language proficiency tests in this evaluation study, it turned out that the results of these tests yielded a number of interesting features.

Methodologically the analyses that were presented showed that it is possible to apply language tests in a meaningful way, even when the experimental group is very small. The introduction of different kinds of control data in the research design has made it possible to evaluate and interpret the scores of the experimental group in a meaningful manner. The use of numerous tests has at least partly reduced the influence of idiosyncratic variation in individual test results on the general evaluation of children's proficiency.

The fact that a number of tests were constructed for younger children than the ones we had in the experimental group created a number of serious problems for the interpretation of the data in terms of group results. With the use of factor analysis we were able to overcome this problem to some extent and deduce some valuable information from these tests.

With respect to the central questions of the evaluation project (section 1), the results of the analysis of the data certainly warrant a positive evaluation of the acquisition of Dutch of the children enrolled in the Foyer bicultural programme. It turned out that only one of the six children clearly showed a proficiency that is considerably lower than that of his Belgian classmates. For the others, differences in proficiency could be detected, but it seemed unlikely that these differences were such that they would impede a successful transition to secondary education.

The main outcome of the part of the evaluation project reported on in this article that can be put to use for the improvement of the bicultural programme is the discrepancy with the Italian children between fragmentary linguistic knowledge and integrated proficiency. Taking into account the peculiar position of Dutch in the overall communicative activities of the children (cf. section 2), it is not surprising that the more integrated application of proficiency should cause them problems. These problems are certainly generally acknowledged by Foyer as well as by the teachers who work in the bicultural project. The observed discrepancy, therefore, is not so much interesting because it signals this problem, but because it offers insights into the effect of possible remedial efforts that can be made. It is clear that the lack of general communicative competence surfaces in the making of mistakes with separate linguistic elements. These mistakes are often interpreted as evidence of the fact that the children who make them do not know the elements they use incorrectly. As a consequence this diagnosis triggers a rather structural approach to the remediation of the observed deficiencies. Our research has shown that the problems that are observed should not be interpreted in terms of knowledge but rather in terms of application of that knowledge. Although the structural approach to language teaching within the bicultural model undoubtedly has important merits (it has, after all, brought about a quite remarkable level of proficiency), it cannot serve as a substitute for more communicatively oriented approaches. We believe that these kinds of approaches would enable the children to make more of the knowledge they have acquired. For this purpose it is equally important to adapt the teaching practice to this insight as to step up the efforts to confront the children with 'living Dutch' outside the classroom and the school.

Of course, the Brussels situation being what it is, it will probably be necessary for a long time to come to give a very important place in the teaching of Dutch to a structural approach. It is, therefore, important to try to attune the curriculum as much as possible to the specific needs of the children. In order to do so, some further research seems necessary. What we have measured are in essence parts of proficiency that appear as teaching subjects in the traditional school curriculum. This curriculum, however, has been designed for teaching in circumstances in which the language acquisition process is externally supported by forms of unguided language acquisition. If the absence of this support needs to be compensated, it will be necessary to investigate with which specific linguistic categories the lack of communicative skills does correlate. It is unlikely, as was indicated in our analyses, that these categories coincide with the areas of proficiency that are traditionally distinguished.

A last point of conclusion concerns the transition of the children from a bicultural primary school to secondary education. We indicated that we believed that most of the children had the necessary proficiency to make that transition. We based this indication mainly on the comprehension skill of these children and on their ability to express themselves. We also pointed out, however, that most of them had problems with the application of linguistic norms. This has as a consequence that, although they are able to follow courses, they may run into problems in instances in which normative matters are central to the judgement of their achievement. If this problem becomes so important that it makes them fail in secondary school, it seems to us that in that case the secondary school system is more at fault than the proficiency of the children.

References

APPEL, R. and MUYSKEN, P. 1987, *Language Contact and Bilingualism*. London: Edward Arnold.

BRUS, B. and VAN BERGEN, J. 1972, *Schriftelijke Opdrachten*. Nijmegen: Berkhout testmateriaal B.V.

DEPREZ, K. 1982, *Naar een eigen identiteit*. Doctoral dissertation, K.U. Leuven.

FILLMORE, L. 1982, 'Instruction language as linguistic input: second language learning in the classroom.' In I. WILKINSON (ed.), *Communication in the Classroom*. London: Academic Press, 283–291.

GREEN, J. and WALLAT, C. (eds), 1981, *Ethnography and Language in Educational Settings*. New Jersey: Ablex Publishing Corporation.

JASPAERT, K. 1986, *Statuut en structuur van standaardtalig Vlaanderen*. Leuven: Universitaire Pers.

KERKHOFF, A. and VALLEN, T. 1984, *Nederlands als tweede taal en schoolsucces aan het einde van de basisschool*. Tilburg Papers in Language and Literature: Katholieke Universiteit Brabant.

KOHNSTAMM, G. and SANAVRO, F. 1983, *De Utrechtse Taalniveau test voor 4–7 jarigen: UTANT*. Lisse: Swets & Zeitlinger.

LEMMENS, G. and JASPAERT, K. 1987, *Evaluatie van het Nederlands in het Foyer-bicultureel onderwijsproject*. Tilburg, internal report.

MEHAN, H. 1985, 'The structure of classroom discourse'. In T. VAN DIJK (ed.) *Handbook of Discourse Analysis, vol. 3: Discourse and Dialogue*. London: Academic Press, 119–131.

OLLER, J. 1979, *Language Tests at School*. London: Longman.

RIVERS, W. 1976, *Speaking in Many Tongues: Essays in foreign-language teaching*. Rowley, Mass.: Newbury House.

VAN ELS, T. *et al.* 1984, *Applied Linguistics and the Learning and Teaching of Foreign Languages.* London: Edward Arnold.
VAN GEERT, P. 1977, 'De grammaticale analysetest (GAT)'. In M. SPOELDERS (ed.), *Pedagogische psycholinguistiek.* Gent: Seminarie voor experimentele psychologische en sociale pedagogiek, 29–48.

3 Language in Immigration: Creativity and Linguistic Mobility

LOREDANA MARCHI

In this chapter, we shall examine the interplay between language and immigration, with reference to the Italian community. We shall see that the process of immigration is related to the process of language development and creativity in language. We shall argue that immigration has a creative impact on language, which is in turn a condition for a successful outcome to immigration. Finally we shall argue that such success is also dependent on schooling, and in particular the influence of school on the linguistic socialisation of the child.

Linguistic Creativity

The creative production and development of a language by a community is particularly evident in an immigration context. This can be seen by contrasting two approaches:

— from a purist linguistic point of view there appear in the language many grammatical errors, interferences and imperfect syntactic constructions;

— from a creative linguistic viewpoint, seeing language as an expression of a community's situation, there is creativity in certain words developed during immigration, e.g. '*chomaggio*' ('*disoccupazione*' — unemployment), '*tartina*' ('*panino*' — sandwich).

Some sentence constructions could be considered erroneous, from a purist viewpoint:

57

— '*voglio bene farlo*' ('*lo voglio fare*' — I want to do it).
— '*ho niente fatto*' ('*non ho fatto niente*' — I have not done anything).
— '*possolo dire*' ('*lo posso dire*' — I can say it).

These are nonetheless linguistic realities, sometimes arising in the heat of the moment, sometimes clearly established in speakers' linguistic repertoire. Both instances are, however, cases of linguistic creativity which are as valuable and valid as that of the community of origin in a non-immigration context. In our view, a linguistic heritage should be considered a source for creativity, by which we mean the speakers' ability to overcome obstacles posed by a language, shifting to a new code which allows greater creativity.

Women in immigration are an extremely important link, even though, since they are often excluded from the world of employment, it would seem that they participate less in the sociocultural reality of the receiving (foreign) country. However, it is known that certain cultural values are transmitted specifically through women.

Even linguistically, the woman's role seems to us extremely important.

We would therefore like to emphasise linguistic creativity in three particularly feminine spheres:

— the relation with the school environment,
— the world of food and cooking,
— the affective domestic sphere.

In the areas of these realities we witness the creation of numerous neologisms and, with high feminine involvement, we find considerable creativity:

— '*cartable*' ('*cartella*' — schoolbag), '*punti*' ('*voto*' — marks)
— '*una cucca*' ('*dolcino*' — pastry), '*suppa*' ('*minestra*' — soup)
— '*demenaggio*' ('*trasloco*' — removal), '*allocazioni familiari*' ('*assegni familiari*' — family allowance).

Linguistic Mobility

Linguistic mobility is another aspect of the linguistic competence of immigrant people. For example, it is interesting to note the systematisation operated on interferences and linguistic interdependences of one code with another. These can vary from the lexical to the syntactic in both immigrant children and adults.

In adult immigrants, we can observe creativity induced by the dominant language, while in children the creativity is obtained from the juxtaposition of both languages. We have to recognise that linguistic creativity during immigration is at its highest when the immigrant person has to face more complex linguistic realities.

Belgium — and particularly Brussels as a bilingual city — offers good examples of this contrast between adults and children. The child is conscious of and reacts to the different languages in his environment. The adult immigrant simply endures the situation. In this case the kind of linguistic mobility involved is inappropriate and inadequate.

The kind of linguistic mobility which is required is represented by the ability of the learner to produce the same thought in several linguistic codes, without the underlying thought being impoverished or undermined. As long as the code is accessible to all those involved it can be changed to suit the situation and the speaker. In a more general sense, the process of integration has to be seen as cultural change and mobility (Leman, 1987: 154–164). Situations in which switches are made to suit participants and context are best understood as evidence of linguistic mobility. For example, there are situations in which the community language will take over from the majority language, e.g. even where there was no employment experience in the country of origin, the mother tongue will still be used in work situations. The original linguistic code will 'interfere' with the code of the host country, which in this example will service the work environment.

The notion of linguistic mobility also requires a different approach to the issue of a language's affective influence. Although the idea of a 'mother tongue' is difficult to define, it nonetheless carries the expression of affective attachment to a language, especially in contexts where a code is not acquired to an adequate level of competence. For example, in the Italian-speaking — or rather Italian dialect-speaking environment of the bicultural project, everyone feels Italian. Yet how many feel a real tie with the Italian language? Each has an individual and very often difficult linguistic history.

People have had to confront different registers which they have only learnt inadequately. Such people remain more affectively bound to what they believe they know best and to that which is tied to the intimate affective sphere, and their childhood memories. From this arises a spontaneous association with the 'mother tongue'. Although this language may not be known well, it remains important for them and has a determining influence on the learning of other languages. Hence it is important for a child to begin formal learning in the mother tongue, which will help the child's educational progress.

It is not simply a question of the number of hours of learning in each language in a bicultural programme. There are more important factors. Many parents themselves feel reassured when their child attends (preferably from nursery class) a school in which the teacher uses the same language as the child's mother. It is not only the teacher's language which is important. She has to talk to, reprimand, hold the child in a similar way to the mother, if this reassurance of all concerned is to be achieved. The figure of the nursery class teacher is extremely important for parents. Often mothers do not think of nursery class as a real school, but change their mind when their own child has to enter one. It is an important step, as the first separation for the child, and it is less traumatic when there is continuity, both linguistic and cultural, between home and school.

Linguistic mobility becomes evident also through the transposition of various terms to family life. A first generation immigrant person, or a second generation child, will not attempt any more to make linguistic translations, as he/she will be inclined to build a new terminology in the dominant language of the situation. For example, Italians in Belgium will speak of '*tartine*' instead of '*panini*' (sandwiches), even if the vehicle language is Italian. It should be known that the great majority of Italian immigrants in Brussels are of Sicilian origin; they therefore have a reduced familiarity with the original language. The initial restricted linguistic condition has caused the phenomenon of 'pidginisation'.

The first generation immigrant usually does not possess an education that will allow him/her to learn another linguistic system. The result is a variety which is almost exclusively lexical, with a minimum quantity of morphology and practically non-existent syntax. The use of this system is of an inexorably reductive kind. We therefore feel authorised to use the word 'pidgin' with regards to this means of communication. There is however a difference. Pidgin is used by South Seas populations as a cohesive medium in some specified situations (commercial settings) among 'equals', while the immigrant uses pidgin not as a cohesive language but rather in positions of inequality. The difference from a linguistic point of view is clear: both morphology and syntax develop in such a way as to allow the use of a creole of immigration. The upper stage reached in this situation is a linguistic structure in which there are numerous words from the new language, but which depends on both the latter and the original language for its structures. This causes numerous interferences.

The process of pidgin formation is an important linguistic process in immigration. When does the phenomenon of pidgin formation occur, and what are its consequences for the language system? In every case there must exist a state of absolute necessity which cannot be resolved in any other way. Pidgin formation is an extreme example of linguistic mix, and pidgins contain elements of all the languages from which they develop. On the other hand, pidgin languages are characterised by certain elements resulting from the actual process of their birth, and from their much limited function as contact languages. Syntax, morphology and phonology are simplified, resulting in an impoverished linguistic heritage. The expressive abilities of a pidgin are limited, since it is not a natural language with a complete range of registers. The important feature of pidgin languages is that they are never mother tongues: pidgin is by definition a second language which is learnt and used in a contact situation. Appel, Hubers and Meijer, at the end of their essay on pidgin languages, add:

> According to some, the initiation of pidgin formation is found in Western Europe, in workers when they speak the language of the country they have moved to. (1979: 194)

There are, however, some few people for whom the pidgin has become the mother tongue. In this situation, and because of the multilingual character of Brussels, we have attempted to ascertain immigrants' attitudes towards the languages co-existing in Brussels. It is possible that parental attitudes towards one or other of the languages will affect children's attitudes towards learning the languages. We are also concerned to know which languages are socially dominant and which subordinate. By 'dominant' we mean here the language which allows socialisation into the culturally and historically superior group; and by 'subordinate', the language which allows socialisation into a culturally and socially isolated group. For Italian immigrants there already exists a dualism in their linguistic heritage, in which the dominant language is standard Italian and the subordinate language is dialect. In this context those who speak pidgin or 'pidginised' dialect are even more disadvantaged than those speaking dialect.

Many immigrant people are confident only in the subordinate language from their original situation, and are already to be considered as potential 'adults of silence', the latter having been so well described on different occasions in recent Italian linguistic and pedagogical history by De Mauro and Don Milani. It is hard for these 'adults of silence' to achieve on their own, in an immigration context, the liberation from such a condition for their children. Only those immigrant people who do not despise their original cultural heritage and try to transmit it to their children, will be able to make them exit from this 'silence zone', by allowing them to assimilate it in an appropriate manner. This cultural transmission is the meaning of certain bi-cultural experiences.

We know by experience that some situations demand the use of a particular language, and that often a pupil will not hold the key to the different linguistic codes which different situations will drive him to use. Therefore, it is vital to take up a perspective of conscious linguistic mobility; that is, the pupil should be competent and conscious of the various codes that he/she will have to employ in a multilingual context. The passage through the mother tongue is possibly the most natural. This is true even if in many cases the mother tongue is not a unitary linguistic construct but a fragmentary patchwork, representing a complex but rich linguistic reality.

The Linguistic Impact of an Integration-oriented Schooling Project

It seems to us that a real integration process can only occur if it involves the school. For the concept of integration, we draw on Schermerhorn (1970), who believes that integration is the process by which societal units or subdivisions are actively and appropriately included in the dominant group's goals and activities. Integration may necessitate a weakening or assimilation of various subdivisions, resulting in the latter's disappearance into the dominant mass or into other subgroups. Assimilation may be a part of the integration process but it is not a necessary condition. A minority group could possibly find a compromise with the dominant majority, to achieve some kind of segregation, resulting in the relatively independent progress of culture and education.

The immigrant parents tend to believe that a schooling process is a process of better integration, often resulting in better insertion into reality, and if we consider the group of Italian parents taking part in the bicultural education project, we can observe this desire in a very definite manner. The immigrant parents are usually confronted with a schooling process in a language differing from their own. If the parents have a limited level of schooling, they will feel more insecure about entrusting the children to an unfamiliar system. This insecurity is compounded when the language in the system differs from their own. In a way, the parents undergo a second immigration: they will try to achieve a more profound integration through their children.

Observing the group of Italian parents, one would say that the above phenomenon commonly occurs, and for some it is a more conscious process than for others. It is, however, clear that parents look upon their children at the end of elementary education with much satisfaction: this stems from the children's ability to speak various languages. Their satisfaction is especially observable with regard to languages to which they have the most emotive reactions. These can be mother tongues or the languages which they must feel have caused their own exclusion, in this case Dutch in Brussels. It is important to study how parents relate to multilingual schooling. The parents are tempted to convey all the affective charge onto one language, this usually being their mother language.

In this situation, a multilingual teaching programme beginning with the mother tongue can produce highly positive results:

— children seem much more secure both in communication and in their relationships,

— children are helped to communicate in different languages and are conscious of which linguistic register is to be used according to context and interlocutor,

— children have both a strong cultural identity and a sense of group membership,

— the choice of Italian as the language of literacy in the first school year confirms Italian as mother tongue but does not make integration in objective cultural terms more difficult; nor does it create a separatist ethnic group (Leman, 1987: 124–139).

This latter point is made from a global interpretation of the process of immigration. In effect the process of ethnic group formation is just the reverse. This means that by reinforcing cultural identity, whilst avoiding social exclusion, a more adequate and harmonious integration can be not only hoped for but actually achieved.

References

APPEL, R., HUBERS, G. and MEIJER, G. 1979, *Sociolinguistiek*. Utrecht: Het Spectrum.
LEMAN, J. 1987, *From Challenging Culture to Challenged Culture*. Leuven: Leuven University Press.
SCHERMERHORN, R. A. 1970, *Comparative Ethnic Relations. A Framework for Theory and Research*. New York: Random House.

4 Mother Tongue Literacy and the 'Shaping' of Knowledge: The Experience of the Italian Children

MARCEL DANESI

Introduction

An issue that seems to crop up persistently when discussing the most desirable form of education for minority-language children concerns the role to be played by the mother tongue in the schooling process. Does the knowledge of the mother tongue handicap the child educationally by delaying the attainment of the high levels of school-language proficiency needed to succeed in a structured academic environment? Or, on the other hand, can this very knowledge be exploited in some meaningful way in order to help the immigrant child learn the school language efficiently and succeed in school from the very outset?

The first question can be seen to crystallise the fears of those who subscribe to what are often called 'deficit theories' (e.g. Gordon, 1981). These attempt to account for differential educational achievements in linguistic terms. A typical articulation of this viewpoint is the one by George Thompson (1952:67) who, in a textbook on child psychology widely used during the 1950s and 1960s, painted the following bleak picture:

> There can be no doubt that the child reared in a bilingual environment is handicapped in his language growth. One can debate the issue as to whether speech facility in two languages is worth the consequent retardation in the common language growth of the realm.

64

The second question can be seen to give expression to a school of thought which sees language systems in the bilingual child as 'interdependent', and as contributors to an enriched form of cognition (e.g. Cummins, 1979, 1984). In their famous 1962 study, Peal and Lambert were among the first to articulate this perspective, describing the functionally bilingual child as (1962: 128):

a youngster whose wider experiences in two cultures have given him advantages which a monolingual does not enjoy. Intellectually his experience with two language systems seems to have left him with a mental flexibility, a superiority in concept formation, a more diversified set of mental abilities.

Who is right? Certainly, the plethora of psychological research on bilingualism that has come forth since Peal and Lambert's seminal study would seem, when considered cumulatively, to support the interdependence hypothesis. But doubts still seem to linger *vis-à-vis* the feasibility of utilising the immigrant child's L1 to remedy deficiencies in the school language. It is, therefore, primarily by closely scrutinising experimental models of education which intentionally build the immigrant child's L1 into their curricular design that it will be possible to resolve the 'deficit vs. interdependence' debate once and for all. Since the Foyer Project was conceived in 1981 as an experiment in mother tongue maintenance (see Leman's chapter in this book for an overall description of the Project), it can be seen to constitute a test case for the interdependence hypothesis. In April of 1987, I was able to collect data on the language characteristics of those children of Italian background enrolled in the Project. The results emerging from my research on these children have been analysed and discussed elsewhere (Danesi, 1987, in press). In the present study, I shall attempt to provide a theoretical framework within which to locate the positive results that emerged from my research. Specifically, I shall relate them to the interdependence hypothesis and to the development of literacy in the mother tongue.

The Interdependence Hypothesis: A Synopsis and a Modification

Before discussing my results, it is useful to review, synoptically, the so-called interdependence hypothesis. As formulated by Cummins (e.g. 1979, 1984), it claims that proficiency and skill in *both* the mother tongue *and* the school language are interdependent. Cummins has articulated this hypothesis formally as follows (1984: 143):

To the extent that instruction in Lx is effective in promoting proficiency in Lx, transfer of this proficiency to Ly will occur provided there is adequate exposure to Ly (either in school or in environment) and adequate motivation to learn Ly.

Despite some valid critiques of various aspects of this hypothesis (e.g. Genesee, 1984; Canale, 1984; Troike, 1984), there seems to be a consensus among most researchers in the field that it constitutes, at the very least, a useful framework for researching, assessing and understanding all kinds of linguistic and cognitive behaviours as they manifest themselves in educational contexts that involve minority-language children. The most salient weakness of this hypothesis, as Wald (1984) has convincingly argued, is its lack of sufficient consideration of the powerful effects literacy has on proficiency levels and on cognitive growth. In order to take this aspect into account, the hypothesis can be modified slightly as follows:

> To the extent that instruction in Lx is effective in promoting proficiency *and literacy* in Lx, transfer of this proficiency *and literacy* to Ly will occur provided there is adequate exposure to Ly (either in school or in environment) and adequate motivation to learn Ly.

By adding the italicised words, the intent is to make explicit the hypothesis that the attainment of literacy in the mother tongue is a determinant of global language proficiency (i.e. proficiency in the mother tongue and in the school language) and, ultimately, of academic achievement. In concrete terms, this modified hypothesis implies that the Italian-speaking children enrolled in the Foyer Project, who have been allowed to develop literacy in their mother tongue from the very outset of their schooling experience, have automatically transferred their literacy skills to the development of proficiency and literacy in both Dutch and French (the school languages). Mother tongue literacy, as will be argued shortly, can thus be seen to constitute a crucial factor in giving the children's three codes (Italian, Dutch, French) the necessary autonomous cognitive status needed for the efficient acquisition of knowledge.

The Language Characteristics of the Italian Foyer Children

The questions I sought to answer in my research on the Italian Foyer children were the following (Danesi, in press):

— To what extent do the codes (Italian, Dutch, French) which the children are acquiring formally at school interfere with each other; or to what extent do they reinforce each other?

— To what degree have the children developed the ability to differentiate and contextualise their codes?

— What overall socio-affective effects has the simultaneous acquisition and functional utilisation of the three codes had on the children?

The method used in obtaining the necessary data to answer such questions consisted in visiting the classrooms in which the children were taught Italian (L1) and mathematics in Italian (L1). The idea was to capture on cassette tapes the spontaneous interactions between the teacher and the children, and among the children themselves. At the conclusion of each visitation, the children were asked to write brief texts (e.g. paragraphs about themselves, questions they might have wanted to ask me about myself or my own country, Canada). In this way, I was able to collect both vocal and written samples of their speech characteristics. The visitations allowed me as well to interview the children and, therefore, to ask them questions pertaining to the uses made of each code, to the perceptions each code evoked, etc.: e.g. 'When and where do you speak Italian, Dutch, French?' 'Which language do you use with your parents, friends, teachers?' 'Which language do you think you speak best and why?' I was also able to interview the teachers of Italian, the teachers who taught them their school subjects, and various educators involved in the Project. This allowed me to obtain both information and opinions on the children's global language proficiency, academic performance, and relationship with their Dutch-speaking peers.

The method used was, obviously, not intended primarily to obtain quantitative data, although some quantification of interference patterns has been possible (as will be shortly discussed). The main aim was to gather enough data on the children's actual speech abilities in their L1 on the basis of communication samples, and then to relate these abilities to the information I was able to collect on their global language proficiency, academic characteristics, and interpersonal qualities. In this way, it has been possible to come up with a broad and representative psycholinguistic profile of the children. The recordings allowed me to get some indication of what Cummins calls 'basic interpersonal communication skills', or BICS (e.g. 1983). Because I was given access to psychometric data (e.g. Coppens, 1985; De Smedt, 1985; Leman, 1985; Spoelders, 1985; Spoelders, Leman & Smeekens, 1985), I have also been able to relate my findings to what Cummins (1983) calls the 'cognitive-academic language proficiency', or CALP, of bilingual children.

The research method used is in line with recent approaches to the assessment of the language and educational problems of the bilingual and bicultural child (e.g. Erickson & Omark, 1981; Rivera, 1983). The 'observational' focus inherent in such approaches provides the researcher with a framework for collecting information on the speech behaviours utilised to negotiate meaning in common situational contexts. Such information cannot be acquired by experimental methods as such. However, the experimental data to which I had access have allowed me to complete the specific details of my psycholinguistic profile.

The findings relative to the three questions posed above will now be summarised. Above anything else, the data collected reveal a remarkably low amount of interference characteristics in the children's three codes. The 'directionality' of interference seems to be almost exclusively from French to Italian. Excluded from consideration are the predictable developmental errors that characterise language acquisition in all children (Locke, 1981). It is not surprising to find that the version of the L1 to which the children are exposed at home is, in general, a dialectal or regional variant of Italian. This is consistent with findings in other areas of the world where there are large settlements of Italian immigrants (e.g. Villata, 1980; Danesi, 1974, 1985a, 1985b). The dialectal characteristics present in the child's linguistic make-up produce a form of L1 competence that lies somewhere on the dialect vs. standard language continuum.

A somewhat unexpected finding in the data is the negligible amount of interference from Dutch to Italian that surfaced in over six hours of recorded speech (a few lexical items), with none being found in the written texts. A plausible explanation for this is that Dutch has not penetrated the modes of thought and the patterns of conceptualisation that would constitute a potential source of interference in the children's other two codes. As borne out by the interview sessions with the children, Dutch plays a minor role in life outside the school environment. It is a language used to learn their school subjects and to interact with their Dutch-speaking teachers and peers while at school. Outside this environment Dutch ceases to play any role in their lives. It constitutes, arguably, an abstract code — a kind of 'academic software' — whose function is perceived to be exclusively school-related. The few children who said that they used Dutch at home did so because one of their parents was Dutch-speaking. One grade five girl remarked, anecdotally, that she would use Dutch at home with her sister only when she did not want her mother to understand what was being said. Despite the low socio-affective value of Dutch for the Foyer children, they have nonetheless developed appropriate levels of literacy in this language. From the psychometric data mentioned above and from the interview sessions with the teachers, I was able to determine, in fact, that, while the Foyer children lagged predictably behind their Dutch-speaking peers in both discourse and literacy-related skills in the early grades, by the later grades they had virtually eliminated the differential gaps.

It is significant to note that such findings are compatible with the general findings on minority-language children. The research shows that immigrant children require, on average, five to seven years to approach grade norms in L2 academic and literacy skills, yet show peer-appropriate L2 communication skills about two years after arrival in the host country (e.g. Cummins, 1984:

130–151). The Foyer experience, therefore, further emphasises the need to take into account both the CALP (literacy-related skills) and BICS (discourse skills) dimensions of language proficiency in any assessment procedure.

To quantify the amount of interference detected in the oral and written data collected, it was first of all necessary to differentiate pure interlingual errors from developmental ones. The literature on the subject of errors has made it saliently obvious that this is a rather difficult analytical task. Nevertheless, it is my view that in bilinguals one cannot ignore interlingual interference mechanisms: their errors can be seen to stem either from an incomplete knowledge of one of the language systems or from firmly entrenched verbal modes of thought in one language that will be transferred unconsciously to the other language. Some errors will, of course, result from an overlapping of these two categories. The 'rule of thumb' I used in assigning a particular error token to an interlingual source was based on the principle of exclusion: i.e. it became a candidate for assignment to an interlingual error category if it could not be explained plausibly in any other way. Therefore, error patterns such as the use of the uvular phoneme /R/, the umlauting of vowels (e.g. /ü/), the use of the second person plural forms for polite address, and the use of lexical items such as *le persone* (instead of Italian *la gente*), *il magazzino* (instead of Italian *il negozio*), can really only be explained in terms of French interference on the L1 (a detailed description of the error patterns can be found in Danesi, in press).

Before looking at the quantitative details of the interference characteristics, a few general observations are in order. Perhaps the most significant finding to emerge from the data is that there is a low interlingual error density in the children's L1. I was not able to identify any instance of a fossilised error pattern that might constitute a serious psycholinguistic obstacle to the formal acquisition of discourse and literacy skills in the L1. Adopting Burt and Kiparsky's (1972) terminological dichotomy of *global* errors (which affect the interpretation of whole sentences and utterances) vs. *local* errors (which affect only an item within a word, phrase, clause or sentence), it can be said that only errors of the local variety were detected in the data.

A rather surprising finding emerged regarding the low density of dialectal interference. This contrasts with findings in parallel socio-educational contexts (e.g. Tosi, 1984; Danesi, 1986). A plausible reason for this might well be that the structure of the Foyer child's educational experience is such that it forces the child to reflect consciously on the differences between the school and home versions of the L1.

As for the influence of the L1 on Dutch and French, I was able to establish from previous studies (e.g. Coppens, 1985; De Smedt, 1985; Leman, 1985; Spoelders, 1985; Spoelders, Leman & Smeekens, 1985) and from teacher interviews that the L1 produces virtually no interference influence on Dutch or French. I was given samples of the children's written work in these languages and I indeed found only the odd trace of the L1 in it.

The quantitative method used to get some indication of the density of interference is a simple one. The number of errors identified in all speech samples at my disposal (including the written work in Dutch and French supplied by the teachers and analysed with their help) is expressed as a percentage ratio to the total number of appropriate forms. This ratio gives us the density of the error types. Thus, the phonological and graphemic densities are expressed as a ratio of the number of phonological or graphemic error tokens found in the individual words to the total number of words; the morpho-syntactic density is expressed as a ratio of the number of morpho-syntactic errors to the total number of sentences; and the lexical density is expressed as a ratio of the number of lexical errors to the total number of words. When the error source is not clear, the either/or designation is used (e.g. *French/Dialect*). The densities are given as rounded-off decimal percentages (e.g. 0.25 = 25%). Table 1 summarises the densities: PD = phonological density; GD = graphemic density; MSD = morpho-syntactic density; LD = lexical density; I = Italian; D = home dialect; FR = French; FL = Dutch/Flemish; nd = no density or density below 0.01.

The most striking pattern that can be extrapolated from the distribution of densities over the grade axis is, clearly, the attrition of all densities towards the later grades. Also rather conspicuous is the lack of interference from Italian on the school codes. Since these densities are derived from all the corpora at my disposal (six hours of recorded conversations, numerous examples of the children's written work, etc.), they can be seen to constitute a fairly good indication of the degree to which the children are able to keep their three codes cognitively differentiated. This was also borne out by a pattern that typified my classroom visitations: as soon as the teacher would point out a particular error committed by one of the children, that very same child showed not only the ability to correct the specific error token, but also to provide a suitable explanation of the source of error.

The opportunity to complete my psycholinguistic profile was given by the interview sessions. These allowed me to pose the appropriate questions aimed at addressing the two remaining research issues mentioned above: namely, the degree to which the children have differentiated and co-ordinated their codes, and the socio-affective effects the formal acquisition of three codes has had on them.

TABLE 1 *Interference Densities Based on Foyer Data*

Inter-ference Source	Grade 1				Grade 2				Grade 3				Grade 4				Grade 5				Grade 6			
	PD	GD	MSD	LD	PD	GD	MSD	LD	PD	GD	MSD	LD	PD	GD	MSD	LD	PD	GD	MSD	LD	PD	GD	MSD	LD
F on I	0.32	0.23	0.18	0.38	0.31	0.19	0.11	0.25	0.21	0.12	0.09	0.14	0.14	0.07	0.04	0.10	0.08	0.01	0.01	0.03	0.02	nd	nd	0.06
D on I	0.02	nd	—	0.01	—	—	—	—	—	—	—	nd	—	nd	—	—	—	—	—	—	—	nd	—	—
F/D on I	—	—	0.23	—	—	—	0.16	—	—	—	0.08	—	—	—	0.04	—	—	—	0.02	—	—	—	0.01	—
FL on I	nd	nd	nd	nd	nd	nd	nd	nd	nd	nd	nd	nd	nd	nd	nd	nd	nd	nd	nd	nd	nd	nd	nd	nd
I on FL	0.01	0.03	0.04	0.05	nd	0.02	0.02	nd	0.01	0.01	nd	nd	nd	nd	nd	nd	nd	nd	nd	nd	nd	nd	nd	nd
I on FR	0.03	0.02	0.01	0.02	nd	0.03	nd	nd	nd	nd	0.01	nd	nd	nd	nd	nd	nd	nd	nd	nd	nd	nd	nd	nd

— indicates that the density is included in another interference source category)

PD = phonological density; GD = graphemic density; MSD = morpho-syntactic density; LD = lexical density; I = Italian; D = home dialect; FR = French; FL = Dutch/Flemish; nd = no density or density below 0.01.

Actually, the above analysis also provides an answer to the question of code differentiation and contextualisation. Upon entering the school system, the Foyer children are confronted with the task of acquiring and mentally separating three codes with overlapping and intersecting functions. The common area of intersection constitutes both a core of common language abilities and a source of transfer. The latter is responsible for the error patterns mentioned above. This initial state can be characterised as one of compound trilingualism. Through the gaining of literacy in the mother tongue, and its utilisation in literacy-related tasks in the other codes, the common core continues to form a cognitive basis for verbal skill transfer, but it eventually forces the child to recognise language differences consciously and, therefore, to separate them functionally. The end result is a state of co-ordinate trilingualism which will vary in degree, of course, according to predictable individual developmental and cognitive differences. The common core, whose contours have been delineated clearly by the effects of literacy, continues to form a basis for global language proficiency, but it eventually ceases to contribute to language admixture, as the density analysis shows.

The functional contextualisation of the three codes was also borne out by the interview sessions. The children were asked where, when and with whom they used their codes. All gave answers that indicated a pattern of contextualisation. The most prevalent one was the following: Dutch is used with their teachers and their Dutch-speaking peers while at school; Italian is used primarily in the home environment; and French is used in all other contexts.

As for the socio-affective effects produced by the Foyer experience on the children, it became immediately obvious that the children had formed close ties with everybody at the school. Their responses to questions during the interview sessions have made it obvious that they have become well-adjusted to the Brussels environment, and that they have found their overall school experience to have been an extremely positive one. When asked if they liked their school, their teachers, etc. they responded unanimously that they really enjoyed coming to school, both to learn and to play. They obviously have sensed that their mother tongue, and their heritage, have been accorded respect and importance in the school environment.

A Theoretical Assessment

It is obvious that by feeling emotionally comfortable in the school environment, the children are better able to concentrate more easily and effectively on the acquisition of knowledge and of academic skills. But another contributing factor to their overall academic success is, in my view, the gaining of literacy in the mother tongue from the very outset. To use a crude analogy, the literacy-related skills developed in the mother tongue have allowed the child to abstract general notions or 'algorithms' of language structure and function. These, in turn, have been applied to the development of the specific 'softwares' of the other codes. By means of an informal 'translation experiment' that I carried out with the grades one and six, I was able to get a glimpse into this pattern of proficiency. The children in these two grades were given a series of idiomatic/metaphorical Italian sentences to translate into both Dutch and French. Translating such utterances can be seen to force the child to relate referents or mental images across languages, rather than just come up with structurally relatable equivalents. To continue the analogy, the children had to make an adjustment in language softwares. All the children had no difficulty in coming up with French equivalents. The grade sixes showed a similar facility in going from Italian to Dutch. Only a few grade ones showed some hesitancy in finding Dutch equivalents, needing prompting from the teacher present.

L1 literacy for the ethnic child can also be seen to constitute the basis for concept-formation. Specifically, it has allowed the children to develop strategies for classifying, abstracting and storing the incoming information in terms of the linguistic labels of the mother tongue. The 'shaping' of knowledge in this way has, subsequently, made it possible to construct general cognitive schemas that are language-independent. These schemas provide the platform upon which, for instance, mathematical concepts and modes of thought are constructed (Danesi, 1987). A revealing finding in this area is that the Foyer children, who use the L1 to learn mathematics in grade one, have shown no difficulties whatsoever in switching over to Dutch in grade two. During the interview sessions, the children pointed out to me, when asked which language they preferred to learn mathematics with, that 'mathematics is mathematics', no matter what language is used to learn it. Clearly, they had acquired the necessary cognitive schemas for learning mathematics to which they had access through any one of their three codes. The knowledge-shaping dimension of literacy is expressed eloquently by Francis (1987: 102):

When literacy forms a part of experience, then opportunities for learning are extended beyond the bounds of knowledge held and gained by the immediate social group. The whole world becomes accessible. Children begin to look at learning from the perspective of what they have come to know about literacy. The conditions of becoming literate are therefore important for their conceptions of learning.

The claim made here is that it is by becoming literate in the mother tongue that the ethnic child gains access to the world of knowledge most effectively. When compared with a control group (e.g. Italian immigrant children enrolled in schools where the mother tongue is not taught), the Foyer children come far ahead in Dutch and French proficiency by the later grades (Coppens, 1985; De Smedt, 1985; Spoelders, 1985; Spoelders, Leman & Smeekens, 1985). This suggests that, by lacking exposure to the instructional practices that develop literacy in the L1, these children have not had the opportunity to develop a deeper conceptual and linguistic proficiency needed to attain high levels of literacy in the other codes.

Concluding Remarks

The main conclusion to be drawn from the Foyer Project is, clearly, that literacy development in the mother tongue constitutes the primary condition for the development of global language proficiency and for the formation of the appropriate cognitive schemas needed to classify and organise experience. As Vygotsky (1962) has persuasively shown, the process of learning language in a conscious and deliberate manner makes the child aware of language form and how it adapts to, and interacts with, the environment. The bilingual and biliterate child can be considered to be a 'little linguist' who has learned to see the L1 as one particular system among many and to view its forms under more general categories. There really appears to be no alternative theory to explain plausibly the manifested learning behaviours of the Foyer children.

The Foyer model of education of minority-language children is, to use Lambert's (1977) terminology, an 'additive' one. It posits the need to incorporate the L1 in a meaningful way into the child's educational experience. The alternative to this model, supported by deficit educational perspectives, is the 'subtractive' one. This aims to subtract the L1 from the very outset of the schooling process, so that exposure to the school language of instruction can be maximised. The research literature in this domain (e.g. Cummins, 1976, 1978; Toukomaa & Skutnabb-Kangas, 1977) has consistently shown, however, that those children who have not developed a 'threshold' level of proficiency in their mother tongue will be more inclined to experience learning difficulties. The Foyer Project therefore constitutes a solid case in favour of additive models of education. As such, it can be seen to constitute a 'kind of field laboratory' (Spoelders, Leman & Smeekens, 1985: 87) for testing out such models in a concrete way. By giving the mother tongue a meaningful role to play in education, the school system will go a long way towards providing a truly enriching academic experience for minority-language children.

References

BURT, M. K. and KIPARSKY, C. 1972, *The Gooficon*. Rowley, Mass.: Newbury House.
CANALE, M. 1984, On some theoretical frameworks for language proficiency. In C. RIVERA (ed.), *Language Proficiency and Academic Achievement*, 28–40. Clevedon: Multilingual Matters.
COPPENS, M. 1985, Observation sur l'expression française chez des enfants italiens et espagnols. In J. LEMAN (ed.), *Four Years of Bicultural Education in Brussels*, 99–109. Brussels: Foyer.
CUMMINS, J. 1976, The influence of bilingualism on cognitive growth: a synthesis of research findings and explanatory hypotheses. *Working Papers on Bilingualism*, 9, 1–43.
—— 1978, Educational implications of mother-tongue maintenance for minority-language groups. *Canadian Modern Language Review*, 34, 395–416.
—— 1979, Linguistic interdependence and the educational development of bilingual children. *Review of Educational Research*, 49, 222–251.
—— 1983, Language proficiency and academic achievement. In J.W. OLLER (ed.), *Issues in Language Testing Research*, 81–96. Rowley, Mass.: Newbury House.
—— 1984, *Bilingualism and Special Education: Issues in Assessment and Pedagogy*. Clevedon: Multilingual Matters.
DANESI, M. 1974, Teaching standard Italian to dialect-speaking students. *Italica*, 51, 295–304.
—— 1985a, L'insegnamento dell'italiano ai discenti italo-canadesi. *Il Veltro*, 29, 447–454.
—— 1985b, *Loanwords and Phonological Methodology*. Montreal: Didier.
—— 1986, *Teaching a Heritage Language to Dialect-Speaking Students*. Toronto: OISE Press.
—— 1987, Formal mother-tongue training and the learning of mathematics in elementary school: an observational note on the Brussels Foyer Project. *Scientia Paedagogica Experimentalis*, 24, 313–320.
—— in press, Mother-tongue training in school as a determinant of global language proficiency: A Belgian case study. *International Review of Education*.
DE SMEDT, H. 1985, The Dutch language skill of Spanish, Italian and Turkish children participating in the Bicultural Project. In J. LEMAN (ed.), *Four Years of Bicultural Education in Brussels*, 80–91. Brussels: Foyer.
ERICKSON, J.G. and OMARK, D.R. (eds) 1981, *Communication Assessment of the Bilingual Bicultural Child*. Baltimore: University Park Press.
FRANCIS, H. 1987. Learning to Read. *Interchanges*, 18, 97–108.
GENESSEE, F. 1984, On Cummins' theoretical framework. In C. RIVERA (ed.), *Language Proficiency and Academic Achievement*, 20–27. Clevedon: Multilingual Matters.
GORDON, J. C. B. 1981, *Verbal Deficit: A Critique*. London: Croom Helm.
LAMBERT, W. 1977, The effects of bilingualism on the individual. In P. HORNBY (ed.) *Bilingualism*, 15–27. New York: Academic Press.
LEMAN, J. 1985, The Foyer Project: A Brussels Model of bicultural education in a trilingual situation. *Studi Emigrazione*, 78, 254–267.
LOCKE, L. 1981, Issues and procedures in the analysis of syntax and semantics. In J. G. ERICKSON and D. R. OMARK (eds), *Communication Assessment of the Bilingual Bicultural Child*, 43–75. Baltimore: University Park Press.

PEAL, E. and LAMBERT, W. E. 1962, The relation of bilingualism to intelligence. *Psychological Monographs*, 76, Whole No. 546.

RIVERA, C. (ed.) 1983, *Language Proficiency and Academic Achievement*. Clevedon: Multilingual Matters.

SPOELDERS, M. 1985, Psycho-educational language assessment in the Brussels Bicultural Education Project. *ITL: Review of Applied Linguistics*, 67–68, 201–216.

SPOELDERS, M., LEMAN, J. and SMEEKENS, L. 1985, The Brussels Foyer Bicultural Education Project: socio-cultural background and psycho-educational language assessment. In G. EXTRA and T. VALLEN (eds), *Ethnic Minorities and Dutch as a Second Language*, 87–103. Dordrecht: Foris.

THOMPSON, G. 1952, *Child Psychology*. Boston: Houghton Mifflin.

TOSI, A. 1984, *Immigration and Bilingual Education*. Oxford: Pergamon.

TOUKOMAA, P. and SKUTNABB-KANGAS, T. 1977, *The Intensive Teaching of the Mother Tongue to Migrant Children of Pre-school Age and Children in the Lower Level of Comprehensive School*. Helsinki: UNESCO.

TROIKE, R.C. 1984, SCALP: Social and cultural aspects of language proficiency. In C. RIVERA (ed.), *Language Proficiency and Academic Achievement*, 45–54. Clevedon: Multilingual Matters.

VILLATA, B. 1980, Le lexique de l'italien parlé à Montréal. *Studi și Cercetări Linvistice*, 31, 257–284.

VYGOTSKY, L. S. 1962, *Thought and Language*. Cambridge, Mass.: MIT Press.

WALD, B. 1984, A sociolinguistic perspective on Cummins' current framework for relating language proficiency to academic achievement. In C. RIVERA (ed.), *Language Proficiency and Academic Achievement*, 55–70, Clevedon: Multilingual Matters.

5 Return to the Home Country: the 'Necessary Dream' in Ethnic Identity

MICHAEL BYRAM

The purpose of this chapter is to examine the role of the Foyer Model in maintaining ethnic identity. It will focus on the relation between identity and links with the country of origin, and it will analyse the contribution of a bicultural programme to the reinforcement of those links. Discussion of empirical evidence will draw on interviews with parents and children in one of the Foyer projects where Italian is taught.[1] I shall first examine some of the reasons parents give for sending their children to a bicultural programme and then relate these to a discussion of ethnicity and identity. Finally, I shall take one factor in the maintenance of a distinctive identity — the dream of returning to the country of origin — and show how it is supported by the Foyer Model.

Choice of School

Parents' explanations of their reasons for choosing a bicultural school are naturally phrased in terms of their hopes and ambitions for the future.[2]

> Pour le bien de l'enfant . . . on ne sait jamais si on retourne en Italie . . . peut-être on restera en Belgique . . . et plus tard pour le travail, s'il connaît le néerlandais et français . . . c'est bien pour le travail . . . et comme il aura aussi l'italien, il connaîtra trois langues . . . j'aime bien.

Two kinds of advantage are apparent here: having a command of both main languages spoken in Belgium[3] will open up economic opportunities and, second, knowing Italian might be useful should the family ever return to Italy. Some parents mention the latter first and seem to put most emphasis on learning Italian:

> Eh bien pour les cours d'italien . . . si jamais on veut retourner en Italie . . . c'est plus facile . . . et pour le flamand c'est intéressant aussi.

Others perceive the programme as bilingual rather than trilingual, and again emphasise the importance of speaking Dutch if one is to find a good job:

> On a essayé de faire une autre expérience . . . comme c'était une école bilingue, italien et flamand, c'était intéressant, nouveau . . . on était curieux pour voir les résultats . . . c'est peut-être un peu plus difficile pour les enfants . . . mais on voulait voir . . . et comme ici en Belgique si vous voulez trouver un bon emploi il faut connaître le flamand, on n'a pas hésité.

In this latter quotation there is also the awareness that the programme may put extra demands on pupils. Most parents are optimistic but it is clear that not all were without hesitation in committing their children:

> on s'est dit: peut-être ce serait possible . . . mais j'avais peur . . . c'était la première année . . . qu'est-ce qui allait se passer . . . on prenait déjà au départ un risque pour un enfant . . . en flamand . . . et puis, bon, on l'a mis . . . et moi, je suis très content.

It is not light-heartedly that one takes risks with one's children and in the discussion of parental choice and ethnic identity below, it is important to remember how carefully parents thought about the risks.

The question of risk arises in a different form once the decision has been made. The significance of parental support and help for children's scholastic success is a well known phenomenon. It is probably one of the factors which prolong the disproportionately high level of children of highly educated parents in the higher reaches of education. The parents of these children are hindered both by their own lack of education and by their ignorance of Dutch:

> Est-ce qu' il n'y a pas moyen de faire . . . d'avoir des cours supplémentaires pour lui? . . . Allez . . . pour vous dire . . . j'ai pas peur de le dire . . . moi je suis analphabète . . . ma femme, elle sait quelque chose . . . mais moi je ne peux pas l'aider . . .

and another parent:

> C'est surtout quand on doit l'aider que, . . . moi, je suis zéro en flamand . . . et alors, . . . si je pouvais l'aider, il serait peut-être plus

avancé, . . . parce qu'il est un peu en retard maintenant et il doit se débrouiller tout seul.

It is therefore not simply the worry of the initial decision which parents have but a continuing worry about whether they have done the right thing. Of course, this is the kind of worry shared by parents of all kinds, but it is accentuated both by the linguistic dimension and by their social position as immigrants — or perhaps migrants. Only one parent was not worried about the lack of help they could give:

Jusqu'à maintenant ça va, . . . mais plus tard . . . ça me fait quand même un peu peur, . . . mais au fond, je me suis dit: mes parents ne m'ont jamais aidé, . . . et on est arrivé en Belgique, . . . on ne connaissait pas un mot de français et on a dû se débrouiller aussi.

Here is something of the characteristic of the migrant who is determined to succeed and expects his own children to have that same determination.

After these first reasons — which might be termed 'instrumental' in their emphasis on knowledge of the languages as a condition of success in finding work or as an aid to return to the country of origin — parents also refer to the importance of Italian in their own and their children's identity. That that identity is not simple and unchanging is evident from the variety of responses to questions about whether parents feel themselves to be Italian or Belgian. The following extract is particularly explicit:

Et vous vous sentez italien ou belge?
Father: Belge, non . . . on a la nostalgie du pays quoi, . . . si j'avais l'occasion de partir . . . travailler là-bas . . . vivre là-bas . . . dépendre de moi-même et pas de quelqu'un d'autre, alors je dis oui . . .
Mother: finalement, là-bas on se sent aussi étranger.
F: on va là-bas, on est étranger aussi . . . puisque quand on va au pays, on dit les immigrés sont là, . . . on est étranger ici et là, on n'a pas de place quoi,
M: enfin on est habitué au rythme belge, je crois
F: on (ne) fait même plus attention au mot étranger, . . . mais de temps en temps, ça nous prend quoi, . . . des envies, . . .
M: c'est normal, . . . les gens sont plus joyeux là-bas, . . . les gens sont plus relax, . . . le temps fait beaucoup aussi, . . . les gens vivent bien là-bas.

In this kind of situation the practical need for children to speak Italian becomes clear. Whenever they go to Italy on holiday — in many cases, this means each year for most of the summer holidays — the children need to be able to make contacts, play with friends and generally cope with the linguistic demands of their environment. They need to speak to grandparents, cousins and other members of the extended family.

> je ne veux pas qu'elle soit perdue, puisque mes parents ne parlent pas de français, . . . ils ont vécu ici, mais maintenant ils habitent à nouveau en Italie et je ne veux pas que la petite ne puisse pas parler avec eux.

This then leads further to discussion of children's identity. Although we must beware of the inaccuracies of self-reporting, the amount of Italian spoken in the family seems to vary. The terminology of the Foyer Model which refers to Italian as the 'mother tongue' is thus not always acceptable.

In a family where more French than Italian is spoken, the following question was put:

> Pour votre petite fille vous avez choisi l'italien comme langue maternelle? Bien disons que, . . . langue maternelle, . . . effectivement, . . . parce qu'elle est italienne effectivement, . . . je ne voudrais pas qu'elle perde cette langue, . . . mais elle apprend le néerlandais, . . . elle apprendra le français . . . ces langues sont toutes aussi bien pour elle.

It is clear from the hesitations and from the use of 'effectivement' that the speaker is not entirely happy with the phrase 'langue maternelle' but it is just as evident that there is no hesitation about the identity being Italian and that there must therefore be a role for the language in supporting that identity.

It was decided therefore to ask the question in a negative way, i.e. asking people whether they thought it is possible to be Italian without speaking the language.

> Croyez-vous que c'est possible d'être italien sans pouvoir parler l'italien? **Mother**: Il y en a quand-même.
> **Father**: Pour moi, non, . . . parce que quand ils ne parlent pas l'italien, . . . c'est parce que ses parents ne lui ont pas appris l'italien, . . . parce que ses parents ont perdu . . . le contact avec l'Italie, . . . parce qu'ils n'aiment pas l'Italie, . . . ou quelque chose comme ça, . . . si on aime son pays, on a tendance à parler la langue, . . . mais pour moi ce ne sont pas des italiens, mais des belges, . . . et ils ne fréquentent pas les italiens, . . . parce qu'il y a des italiens, qui sont nés ici et qui fréquentent encore les autres italiens . . . et ils parlent l'italien toujours, . . . mais les autres qui ne fréquentent plus les autres italiens, . . . comment voulez-vous qu'ils soient italiens?

This quotation is interesting both because it represents the general awareness that there are people who no longer speak Italian and who are difficult to categorise, and because it suggests that contact with other Italians in Belgium is a condition of remaining Italian. The difficulty of maintaining Italian against the influence of French is recognised, and the role of the school considered to be crucial in the following answer to the same question:

> C'est possible, . . . j'en connais, . . . ce sont des italiens, . . . eux ils parlent très bien l'italien, . . . mais les enfants ne connaissent pas un mot en italien, . . . parce que, . . . les parents ne veulent pas parler italien avec eux ou, . . . les enfants même ne veulent pas le parler, . . . je ne sais pas, . . . et ils n'ont pas la chance d'avoir une école biculturelle tout près, . . . et il y a beaucoup de gens qui m'ont demandé comment elle était l'école, . . . parce qu'ils sont fort intéressés, . . . alors moi, j'ai dit, elle est impeccable cette école.

The difficulty is all the more evident to those parents who speak very little Italian themselves because they were not encouraged to do so by their own parents:

> **Father**: ils n'ont pas vu la nécessité, . . . ils ne réfléchissaient pas comme nous aujourd'hui, . . . c'est une autre époque . . .
> **Mother**: mais nous au début, quand on était marié, . . . et on se retrouvait en Italie, . . . on avait un grand handicap, . . . on s'est dit, . . . c'est pas possible que nous italiens nous ne pouvons pas parler notre propre langue, . . . là on s'est vraiment senti . . !
> **Father**: ça fait mal, . . . on a peur de parler, . . . on se sent pas bien . . .

The position is made more complex by the use of and attitudes to dialect. Most families said that when they speak Italian it is a dialect, although there were those who attempt to speak standard Italian either because they think it better for the children or because they come from different dialect areas and need to speak standard in order to understand each other. It is impossible to know how successful these attempts are and to what degree they approach the standard. Most would, however, probably agree with the judgement expressed in the following:

> Ici à la maison vous parlez italien ou français?
> Mais lui il parle mieux le flamand maintenant, . . . parce que l'italien, . . . malheureusement ici nous parlons parfois le dialecte . . .
> Pourquoi vous dites malheureusement? vous trouvez que ce n'est pas bien?
> C'est mieux de parler le bel italien, . . . c'est comme le wallon et le français . . .
> Et vous parlez souvent italien, dialecte, à la maison?
> Tout le temps.

There is evidence therefore that the instrumental reasons are not the only ones. A good education is seen as a means to a good job and in Brussels this means learning Dutch. A knowledge of Italian could also be useful for a return to Italy and is certainly useful on holiday. In addition, however, learning Italian is fundamental to being Italian, even though 'being Italian' is itself an ambiguous and difficult concept. Choice of a bicultural school is crucial in supporting that identity.

The degree of support required by parents of the school varies according to the extent that their own identity and the identity of the home is firmly established. The relationship between home and school in this respect is complex and to construct a description of the home culture from interviews is a task fraught with difficulties. Two cases give some impression of the range of differences:

Family 1: in Belgium since 1970, both parents about 40 years old, return to Italy every two or three years, still have a grandparent there.

Vous vous sentez belge ou encore italien?
Bien, disons que c'est difficile . . . on a pris toutes les habitudes d'ici . . . mais c'est difficile de dire si on est belge à cause de ça . . . comme c'est difficile de dire que, . . . qu'on n'est pas belge non plus, . . . puisque tous les enfants sont ici . . . alors . . . on est ni l'un ni l'autre . . . ici on est étranger et chez nous on est étranger aussi . . .
Et ici à la maison vous parlez italien? Normalement on parle français, puisque j'ai aussi un autre garçon, . . . alors lui il connaît l'italien . . . de parler, . . . mais pas écrire, . . . et alors on parle français le plus souvent, . . . mais des fois on parle en italien aussi . . .
Et vous, . . . vous n'avez jamais eu envie de retourner en Italie?
Personnellement, non . . . pourtant ma femme aimerait bien retourner, mais moi, . . . je crois qu'il y a des inconvénients . . . enfin dans le temps je suis parti de l'Italie puisque je n'avais pas de travail, . . . enfin on avait du travail mais on n'était pas payé assez . . . pour vivre convenable, . . . parce que du travail on en trouve toujours, . . . donc je suis venu ici et je suis bien traité ici . . . ça me dit rien, . . . enfin oui mais,. . . . c'est une espèce de nostalgie disons, . . . que . . . on a tous . . . c'est pour ça qu'on retourne de temps en temps, . . . mais pour toujours, . . . non . . . et puis si les enfants grandissent ici . . . et nous on retourne là-bas, . . . ils n'ont plus personne ici, . . . c'est comme nous quoi?
Est-ce que vous trouvez qu'ils (les enfants) sont plus belges que vous?
On le remarque tout de suite, . . . nous autres, on a été éduqué

différemment, . . . on essaie de leur donner la même éducation, . . . mais ce n'est pas possible, . . . l'école . . . et tout . . . et . . . ce que nous on n'osait pas, eux ils osent, . . . ils sont plus libres, . . . ce n'est pas une critique, mais une constatation, . . . nous, on n'avait pas cette liberté!
Et quand vos enfants vous accompagnent en Italie, est-ce qu'ils changent, . . . est-ce qu'ils deviennent plus italiens ou . . ?
Les enfants, ils s'adaptent facilement, . . . ils aiment bien aller là-bas, . . . mais à la fin des vacances, surtout la petite elle demande aussi: quand est-ce qu'on retourne en Belgique? . . . pour eux aussi, la nostalgie du pays de leur naissance règne, . . . c'est l'envers . . .

Here is then a family which is firmly implanted in Belgium, speaking French at home but still with some ties to Italy. It is particularly interesting that like many others these parents recognise that their children have a different relationship to Belgium, that they have a different identity. One parent said that it is to be expected that his children are less Italian than himself, and for that reason sends them to Italy every year for three months. This family, however, does not attempt to reverse the process of change and moreover perceives that it is not simply a question of the amount of experience of Italy, but that there are far stronger influences at work in school and elsewhere. The change in ethnic identity is part of a complex change of educational traditions.

Family 2: left Italy 20 years ago, went first to France, both parents about 40 years old, go to Italy every year, grandparents still there.

Mother: on est italien de naissance, mais on vit plus ici que là-bas, . . . mais on tient à notre culture . . .
Father: j'ai étudié en Italie, . . . ma culture est italienne, . . . je reste italien, . . . malgré que j'ai pris la nationalité belge, . . . pour être plus favorisé ici en Belgique, . . . mais je suis italien, ma femme est restée italienne (. . .) nous les italiens, on a une autre culture, . . . ça commence du latin, . . . c'est nous qui avons dominé le monde à ce moment-là, . . . jusqu'à 1300 les gens en Europe parlaient le latin, . . . c'est pour ça aussi que je veux qu'elle sait que l'italien c'est une langue avec une tradition, . . . une culture, . . . on a des poètes, des écrivains, . . . pour moi Dante n'a pas son égal ni en Angleterre, ni en France ou ailleurs, . . . c'est unique, . . . et c'est ça que je veux faire parvenir à mes enfants, . . . la grandeur de la langue italienne . . .

The language of the home is 'le bel italien', partly because the parents are from different parts of Italy and cannot therefore use their own dialects, but partly because the parents wish their children to speak standard Italian. On the one hand there is no intention to return to Italy for good 'si on retournait un jour, . . . on serait aussi perdu là-bas', yet on the other hand the identity remains strong and is uninfluenced by the question of official nationality.

The atmosphere of this home is therefore quite different from the first. There is a determination that the children shall have the same kind of upbringing as the parents, and this is focused on the language and traditional high culture of Italy and its history. This kind of clear statement is unique in the interviews, but it may be that these parents are expressing a feeling about the education of their children which others who feel still very strong ties to Italy would share. Those parents who continue to speak Italian — whether standard or dialect — to their children do so either because their own French is so weak or because they have deliberately decided to do so. But even those whose French is weak have probably made an unconscious decision deliberately to continue to speak Italian, because almost all have been in Belgium long enough to have learnt French if their identity had changed. The fact that they have not done so is an indication of the strength of their ties with Italy and of their Italian identity.

It is clear from these two cases that the relation between home and school will vary from individual to individual. The expectations as to how successful school can be in supporting an Italian identity will also vary. Some parents find the difference between themselves and their children easier to accept. Some see the change as inevitable. It is nonetheless clear that the choice of a bicultural school involves, for many if not most, a hope and expectation that their children will not only acquire useful linguistic knowledge but also support and help in understanding themselves and their own identities. The question now arises as to what kind of identity is involved.

Identity, Ethnicity and the Bicultural School

Discussions with parents, interviewed in French, involved the use of the terms 'Italy' and 'Italian'. In effect parents and children sometimes refine the terms by referring to 'Sicily' and 'Sicilian' — or, in some cases, other specific regions of Italy. The refinement becomes most necessary when talking of language and dialect, for the difference between standard Italian and dialect is one which is very evident and indicative of other less obvious differences.

Such a shift of emphasis is symptomatic of the way in which identity is created. In the first instance the contrast is between being Belgian and Italian, irrespective of the sub-divisions of Belgian and Italian identity. Indeed, for the parents the sub-divisions of Belgian identity have little significance or interest;

speaking Dutch is a useful tool for acquiring a job, not a symbol of Flemish-Belgian identity. On the other hand, parents are more conscious that 'Italian' is too general, for it misses the sense of being a particular kind of Italian, namely Sicilian — and of speaking a particular dialect.

This phenomenon of determining identity by comparison and contrast with others, rather than in an absolute sense, is symptomatic of the marking of ethnic identity by boundary phenomena first clarified by Barth (1969). Barth argues that attempts to define ethnicity in terms of specific and unchanging characteristics misses the point that the ethnic identity of one group is created in the context of other identities. The phenomena which mark the boundaries between one group identity and another will vary from situation to situation and may change over time. Although language is often such a marker, it need not be so (Le Page & Tabouret-Keller, 1985: 215). The fundamental issue is whether an individual or group 'identifies itself, and is identified by others, as constituting a category distinguishable from other categories of the same order' (Barth, 1969: 11). This subjective self-ascription can then be made objective by whatever means are appropriate. A further refinement is cited by Leman. Writing within the Barthian framework, he draws on a distinction between 'ethnic category' and 'ethnic group' (Leman, 1987: 130–1):

one may speak of an ethnic category when there are common ethnic characteristics between members of a group without this leading to common group bonds . . . When, however, people begin to interact meaningfully on the basis of one or more common ethnic traits . . . then one must speak of an ethnic group.

Leman suggests that most Sicilian immigrants experience their ethnicity in the former of these two ways.

It is clear from the interviews cited above that language is one of the boundary markers for these parents. It is also clear that, in some cases, parents are aware that their own knowledge of Italian (standard or dialect) is not adequate for them to be able to mark the boundary themselves, or pass on that ability to their children. The school is seen as a source of such ability, as a means of ensuring that their children can symbolise their Italian identity in language, as well as putting their language to use when in Italy. Furthermore, parents are aware that, unless they take some kind of action, their children's identity will be quite different from their own.

There is some indication of this in interviews with pupils too. Each individual is different, of course, and it is important to look first at a number of cases. Pupils were asked about their abilities and feelings when speaking their languages and also about their identity. The hesitations and, occasionally, inconsistencies in what they say are doubtless a consequence of the interview situation and of the difficulty that many children of 11 or 12 years would have with these questions. There are also, however, indications of their feelings about their ethnc identity.

Consider the following cases:

Pupil 1: speaks at home 'l'italien, aucun dialecte, l'italien, parce que mon père et ma mère ont dit que le dialecte ça te ferait aller la voix pas bien, tandis que s'ils parlaient l'italien avec nous jusqu'à ce qu'on grandissait alors on saurait mieux la langue italienne, mais comme on habite à . . . on habitait à . . . on parlait [indistinct words] le dialecte mais moi je connais seulement quelques mots mais je le parle pas tellement, si quelqu'un d'autre me parle je comprends mais si moi, mais je n'arrive pas moi à le parler'. However, she also later says she speaks French with her parents 'c'est pas beaucoup, et c'est pas quelques mots, c'est entre les deux'. With her siblings she speaks all three languages and, asked about whether she mixed the languages, says 'des fois quand je veux dire par exemple prends le couteau, je dis prends, et en flamand je dis couteau, et quelquefois c'est un mélange des mots'. Asked 'tu te sens différente?' when speaking the three languages she says 'bien quand je parle flamand mais pas le français et l'italien . . . je sais pas bien le prononcer et il y a beaucoup de mots que je comprends pas, chaque semaine il y a des mots que je n'avais jamais entendu et, tandis qu'à l'italien, déjà les mots je les sais presque tous et le français aussi mais il y a quelques mots que ça me revient pas dans la tête'. Yet to the question of 'langue préférée' she says 'non, je les aime bien tous les trois', but as to which she speaks best 'le français et l'italien je parle mieux que le flamand, parce que l'italien et le français, le français je l'ai su à peine que je suis née, l'italien c'est venu à l'école'. Of course, there is some inconsistency in what she says but this is not unusual, and certainly not to be criticised. Her identity is not simple: 'je me sens bien plus italien, mais ici ça me dit d'être belge et italien quand je suis ici, allez, dans ce pays, ça me dit d'être belge [indistinct words]'. Later she says 'c'est à dire que maintenant, avant quand j'étais lá (Italy), pour venir en Belgique, j'avais envie de venir en Belgique, et maintenant que je suis en Belgique j'ai envie de rentrer en Italie'.

Pupil 2: speaks French and Sicilian with parents and a brother ('je parle français avec lui, pas toujours mais plus français que sicilien'). Her preferred language she says is 'français' (et puis?) 'le sicilien mais je connais pas tellement bien encore': of speaking Sicilian 'c'est très, ce n'est pas vraiment comme du français, et c'est très drôle et' followed by silence and an inability to articulate her feelings any further. However, despite

this perception of her ability in Sicilian, she says of her identity 'sicilien
. . . belge aussi, j'aime pas tellement qu'on me dit que je suis belge
parce que, je sais pas pourquoi.' Finally, when asked if learning Italian is
'utile' she says 'oui, parce que je sais pas encore parler le sicilien, donc je
peux parler l'italien'. For her the future lies in Belgium: 'c'est pour le
travail, c'est pour ça qu'on est venu, je crois je vais rester en Belgique et en
vacances aller en Sicile'.

Pupil 3: speaks 'un peu sicilien, un peu français' with parents ('je sais pas
le dire mais un peu moins (français) que le sicilien') and French with
siblings. Her 'langue préférée' is Sicilian which 'me fait penser à la Sicile'
which she does not visit every year, as many others do. With respect to
identity: 'un peu de tout [laughs] je me sens plus belge parce que je suis née
ici, alors' (est-ce que tu te sens italien?) 'pas tellement' (ou sicilien?) 'pas
tellement'. When she does go to Sicily 'je crois pas que je suis en Italie, on
dirait que je suis toujours en Belgique . . . on dirait que je suis pas en
Italie, on dirait que c'est un rêve, je sais pas le dire', again finding the
feelings, not surprisingly, difficult to articulate; as for returning to Italy,
'non, je vais travailler ici'.

Pupil 4: speaks at home 'italien, toujours l'italien' although his father also
speaks dialect which the children understand; later he says 'je me dis
que . . . il y a pas besoin de faire l'italien (at school) parce que nous, à la
maison on parle italien, et si on a des mots faux, ma mère elle les corrige'.
With siblings, however, he speaks all three languages using Flemish with
one sister when they don't want another sister to understand. To the
question of 'langue préférée' he answers 'tous les trois' and says his
'langue maternelle' is 'le flamand et l'italien . . . je sais pas, mais je
préfère mieux l'italien que le français, enfin tous les trois', saying he
speaks Italian best and is quite definitely Italian in identity.

Pupil 5: speaks at home 'plus souvent le français, un peu l'italien et un peu
le flamand avec ma maman' and with siblings all three languages. He
doesn't know which language he speaks best but as to identity 'je me sens
belge, mais je suis italien, . . . parce que je suis en Belgique alors, . . .
des fois aussi je me sens italien.'

When asked if he felt Flemish or francophone Belgian, he said 'tous
les deux'. For him return to Italy is very doubtful and he too talks of
staying in Belgium to work and returning to Italy for holidays. What
images does he hold of Italy? 'Mon pays, ma famille qui est là-bas, mais
moi je suis à la Sicile, tout en bas, alors là il y a peu de gens, mais ici par
exemple il y a beaucoup d'écoles et tout, il y a des hôpitaux, là-bas pas
tellement chic, . . . en Sicile c'est, . . . pour trouver une école

c'est, . . . il faut courir loin, et à un hôpital il faut [indistinct words] par exemple les draps [indistinct words] tu dois apporter de la maison, et tout des choses comme ça, . . . tu dois acheter de la piqure et tout, et tous les choses, parce que là-bas it faut aller loin, et tous des choses comme ça'. He talks of his family and holidays and, when asked how he feels, says 'je me sens plus italien quand je suis là-bas parce que je parle que l'italien, on ne sait pas' (est ce que tu te sens sicilien comme tes cousins) 'non je me sens plus italien parce que des fois je comprends pas qu'est-ce qu'ils disent en italien'.

Pupil 6: speaks both French and Sicilian at home, mainly Sicilian with his mother, mixing in French words when he doesn't know them in Sicilian, but French with siblings. His preferred language is 'sicilien, c'est plus glissant [indistinct words] je me sens mieux tandis que le français, quand je parle, je sais pas, en italien je suis mieux, ça glisse, les mots glissent et ils vont plus vite.' Of identity he says: 'je sais que je suis né ici en Belgique mais je me sens italien et belge' (Qu'est-ce qui est le plus fort?) 'le belge je crois, non quand je dis "viens ici", en sicilien j'aime mieux le dire, "viene cui", (indistinct words) mais maintenant je sais mieux le dire "viens ici" [indistinct words] mélange de sicilien et italien et belge, tout, je sais pas, ça vient tout de suite'. But in Sicily he feels Sicilian and again refers to how when he speaks Sicilian 'ça glisse'. He is the only one who is quite sure he is going to return and has quite definite plans for work. For the moment the images of Italy are: 'c'est beau, quand tu es à la mer, on dirait que tu es au paradis' (L'Italie, ça veut dire quoi pour toi?) 'Ca veut dire que c'est les vacances pour moi, j'aime bien et ça m'amuse, il y a tous les parents là-bas, que j'ai ici, que j'ai seulement cinq par . . , cinq famille, et là-bas il y a beaucoup plus de famille et moi là-bas je m'amuse, tous les mardis il y a le marché . . .'.

There is plenty of evidence in these cases that language is a symbol and an embodiment of identity, for example 'je me sens plus italien quand je suis là-bas parce que je parle que l'italien' (Pupil 6). There is also evidence that children feel pulled from both sides, for example 'j'avais envie de venir en Belgique, et maintenant que je suis en Belgique, j'ai envie de rentrer en Italie' (Pupil 1). They are also concerned about the level of their proficiency in Italian — and in Dutch. Parents are therefore justified in their view that they must provide support for their children by choosing a bicultural school.

It is, however, also evident from the quotations from pupil interviews that visits to Italy are another significant source of support for their identity. For one (Pupil 3) for whom visits are less frequent, they take on a dream-like character and clearly have significant affective influence, which infects her feelings about language. Another (Pupil 6) expresses something similar in his feelings about speaking Sicilian and he doubtless speaks for others when he describes the beauty of Sicily in summer. He is quite convinced that he will 'return' to Italy — despite being born in Belgium — whereas most are sure that their future lies in Belgium. Their reasons are probably influenced by their knowledge of why their parents left Italy: they know they came in search of work. Thus the answer one child (Pupil 3) gives to the question of whether she will 'return' to Italy — a question she accepts as meaningful — includes a reference to work. Another (Pupil 2) is quite explicit — 'c'est pour le travail, c'est pour ça qu'on est venu' — and sees the future as a continuation of her parents' routine of living in Belgium and spending holidays in Italy. To understand more precisely what is meant by 'return', it is necessary to consider what parents say.

The Concept of 'Return'

Since the Foyer Model has the explicit aim of providing pupils with an adequate linguistic and cultural experience for them to return to the country of origin, interviews with parents included discussion of whether they would 'return'. The idea is apparently often discussed by parents and introducing it into the interview immediately provoked response. As pointed out above it is part of the rationale for choosing the bicultural programme.

However, one person said that the linguistic demands of return are perhaps not catered for:

il y a beaucoup de gens du biculturel qui envoient leurs enfants à l'école, espérant de retourner un jour, . . . je crois, . . . mais je crois que, . . . l'italien n'est pas assez instruit là-bas, . . . pour pouvoir retourner, . . . bon je ne dis pas, . . . ils connaissent bien l'italien, . . . mais le cours principal c'est quand même le néerlandais . . . bon, . . . en italien, . . . si je leur demande d'écrire quelque chose en italien, . . . bon, ils le savent, . . . mais ce n'est pas suffisant pour retourner . . .

Others also mentioned the need for knowledge of writing for return, although this was the only one to doubt the level of proficiency.

On the other hand, the overwhelming response to the question of returning one day was that it is something always talked about but it is doubtful if it will ever happen. Some said quite definitely they had no intention of returning:

Ah non . . . je suis venu ici à l'âge de trois ans . . . et je vais y mourir . . . je crois que les enfants vont rester ici aussi . . . alors je ne crois pas qu'on retournera un jour . . . on est bien en Belgique . . . il ne fait pas toujours beau mais . . .

The question of where the children will live is an important one, frequently mentioned. The following parent is aware that he is cut off from his own parents and would not want his children to be in the same position, despite a certain nostalgia and his wife's wish to return:

> Personnellement non . . . pourtant ma femme aimerait bien retourner mais moi . . . je crois qu'il y a des inconvénients . . . enfin dans le temps je suis parti de l'Italie puisque je n'avais pas de travail . . . Donc je suis venu ici et je suis bien traité ici . . . ça me dit rien . . . enfin, oui mais . . . c'est une espèce de nostalgie disons, que . . . on a tous . . . c'est pour ça qu'on retourne de temps en temps . . . mais pour toujours, non . . . et puis si les enfants grandissent ici, et nous on retourne là-bas . . . ils n'ont plus personne ici . . . c'est comme nous, quoi!

There is also an awareness that return is not without problems. They are clearly linked by the following parent with the question of identity raised by the interviewer:

> —Vous vous sentez belge ou encore italien?
> —Bien, disons que c'est difficile, . . . on a pris toutes les habitudes d'ici, mais c'est difficile de dire si on est belge à cause de ça . . . comme c'est difficile de dire que . . . qu'on n'est pas belge, non plus . . . puisque . . . tous les enfants sont ici . . . alors . . . on est ni l'un ni l'autre . . . ici on est étranger, et chez nous on est étranger aussi . . . tous les gens de notre âge . . . toute une génération sont partis de l'Italie . . . alors si on rentre en Italie on est traité comme des étrangers . . . puisque la nouvelle génération nous connaît pas . . . personnellement je suis bien . . . où je gagne ma vie . . . je n'ai rien contre les belges ni contre les italiens.

This poignant description of the fate of a generation which belongs nowhere speaks for many, and again the brief mention of the children demonstrates how parental origin and identity are closely related to and interdependent with the future of the next generation. Even those who are more assertive about their identity fear they belong nowhere:

> finalement là-bas on se sent aussi étranger. On va là-bas, on est étranger aussi, . . . puisque quand on va au pays, on dit 'ah, les immigrés sont là' . . . on est étranger ici et là-bas . . . on a pas de place, quoi . . . enfin, on est habitué au rythme belge, je crois . . . on fait même plus attention au mot étranger . . . mais de temps en temps, ça nous prend, quoi . . . des envies.

The question of adapting to Belgium is often linked to what might appear a superficial problem of climate, but it is also symptomatic of a way of life:

—Et n'aimeriez-vous pas retourner un jour pour de bon?
—Ah moi, toujours . . . ce n'est pas que je n'aime pas la Belgique, . . .
non . . . mais, c'est le temps, je n'aime pas ce temps ici . . . là-bas,
même quand il fait mauvais, il fait chaud.

One couple put it a little more philosophically:

—les gens sont plus joyeux là-bas . . . les gens sont plus relax . . . le
temps fait beaucoup aussi . . . les gens vivent bien là-bas
—Ici tout le monde court, mais on se demande après quoi, au
fond . . . eux, ils sont plus relax.

And there is still a strong sense that there would be a problem of finding work,
the very problem which forced them away:

Nous avions envisagé ça . . . même il y a pas longtemps . . . mais il
n'y a pas beaucoup de travail . . . et il faut avoir au moins son propre
logement . . . et alors pouvoir trouver un petit travail . . . même
demi-temps mais il faut savoir se débrouiller . . . il faut savoir tout
faire . . . puisqu'il est trop tard pour s'implanter là-bas et trouver un
métier fixe.

In some ways, therefore, the whole question of return remains a dream,
something to hope for but not envisaged as a reality.

—Aimeriez-vous retourner pour de bon?
—Pas pour de bon . . . non, . . . plus maintenant, c'est fini . . . que
voulez-vous qu'on fasse là-bas, . . . si on gagne deux millions au
lotto . . . là, on retourne . . . pour le soleil.

And yet the dream does occasionally come true:

mes parents sont retournés aussi . . . puisqu'ils ont eu la chance de
gagner au lotto . . . mon père était malade ici . . . et là, avec le beau
temps, il va bien.

The significance of 'return' lies, however, not in the realisation of the
dream, but in the link with the past and with a homeland. De Vos and
Romanucci-Ross (1975: 17) argue that ethnic identity is past-oriented,
'primarily a sense of belonging to a particular ancestry and origin and of
sharing in specific religion as language'. The parents feel they are cut off from
their ancestry and origins:

Si, j'ai envie de retourner . . . c'est encore toujours mon pays . . . c'est
mon pays . . . ma terre . . . ma mère est là encore . . . même que
. . . ici, c'est bien . . . là-bas c'est mon pays . . . mon enfance . . .
mes parents . . . la famille . . . c'est là-bas
(This particular person had left Italy in 1958, almost 30 years before.)

Yet because their children do not have the same memories of the homeland, they are unable to share their parents' 'nostalgie du pays'. So to return would possibly resolve the feeling of being cut off from older generations and simultaneously cut them off from the following generation. They cannot find a real solution, therefore, and they are, as one parent said, foreign wherever they live.

The resolution which is found is to keep the possibility of return always alive, to talk of it from time to time, whilst knowing that it will never be realised. The consequence can be in some cases a lack of a national identity, a feeling of being considered a foreigner by other people everywhere and therefore accepting that one has no clear identity. In other cases, the doubt is resolved:

> bon, moi je suis née en Belgique . . . je me sens italienne . . . et belge en même temps, quoi . . . je suis vraiment pour les deux . . . j'ai les deux nationalités en moi et quand je vais en Italie . . . je me sens prèsque étrangère je me sens . . . je ne le sais pas . . . je n'ai peut-être pas leur mentalité . . . et alors je me dis . . . dans le fond . . . je me sens plus belge . . . mais mon mari, c'est le contraire . . . c'est peut-être le fait qu'il est venu ici a l'âge de sept ans . . . je ne le sais pas . . .

The Foyer Model and 'Return'

I have argued that for parents the dream of 'return' is a support to their own feeling of being a generation which belongs neither in Belgium nor in Italy. It is in essence a dream which will not be realised because most parents know that their children will not want to return. There is evidence from pupils that this is, for the majority, indeed the case. On the other hand, the Foyer Model aims to provide children with the language and culture which would give them the opportunity to return, and this is seen as an advantage by parents so their children can cope if they do return. They seem therefore to hold mutually conflicting views: that their children will not return to Italy and that they should learn Italian in order to be able to return. This in itself is not surprising. People often hold mutually contradictory views as a means of coping with difficulties and paradoxes in their lives. What is interesting is that — leaving aside the very few exceptions who do in fact return — the Italian version of the Foyer Model is helping to maintain a fiction.

It is a necessary and useful fiction and the learning of Italian has other benefits, too, which have not been discussed here. The term 'fiction' is not therefore to be taken negatively. Indeed, dreams and fictions of all kinds are fundamental to daily life. In this particular case, the fiction reveals an important aspect of ethnic identity and clarifies the distinction between long established European minorities and the new minorities of the mid-twentieth century.

In their account of European 'ethnic and political nations' Krejci and Velimsky (1981: 45) suggest that there are 'objective' and 'subjective' factors in ethnic identity, and consider that 'the subjective factor of (national) consciousness' is the most important. Nonetheless, objective factors are also significant and they isolate five: territory, state, language, culture and history. Not all of these need to be present, but the more there are the stronger the basis for a consciousness of identity. Le Page and Tabouret-Keller (1985: 209) also list a number of criteria which people use to identify ethnic groups: physical features, provenance, language, family descent or race, nationality and culture/tradition/religion. The new minorities of Europe, such as the Italians in Brussels, differ from the 'established' minorities (Churchill, 1986) — such as the German minority of Belgium — in that they do not live in the 'territory' or 'area of provenance' which is a potential characteristic of their identity, a potential boundary-marking phenomenon.

The dream of return — the necessary fiction — thus maintains a fundamental link which marks ethnic identity. Many parents and all the children in this particular study were born in Belgium. One parent cited felt that ultimately this meant that her Belgian identity was stronger. Others, however, use the dream as a support for their Italian identity. In the case of the children, who in general have no dream of return, its significance is much reduced, although they are aware that it is part of their parents' way of thinking. For them, however, it is above all a means of being accepted by people when they are on holiday. They are criticised, as one pupil said, by 'les gens de là-bas' if they cannot speak Italian:

ils se disent italiens mais ils ne connaissent pas d'italien, alors je connais l'italien.

For the children, the holidays in Italy are perhaps a weaker version of the dream of return. One child quoted above saw her future life in Belgium but her holidays always in Italy. It is not only fortuitous that others described their holidays as a dream — even though it is a dream of a different kind — and another described being in Sicily as like being in paradise. These two children articulate a fundamentally significant dimension of immigrant life, which the Foyer Model helps to maintain.

Notes

1. This chapter is based on interviews with all but two of the Italian families sending their children to one of the schools in the Foyer programme. The interviews were carried out by Mr Luc Dierickx who was my research assistant on the evaluation of the programme in the school. Interviews with pupils, carried out in the process of evaluation, were conducted by the author.

2. Transcriptions do not attempt to reflect pronunciation or intonation and are normalised to standard written French. However, hesitations are indicated by three dots, irrespective of length of pause.

3. German is also a recognised language in Belgium, but is spoken only in a geographically restricted area in the east.

References

BARTH, F. (ed.) 1969, 'Introduction', *Ethnic Groups and Boundaries*. London: Allen and Unwin.

CHURCHILL, S. 1986, *The Education of Linguistic and Cultural Minorities in the O.E.C.D. Countries*. Clevedon: Multilingual Matters.

DE VOS, and ROMANUCCI-ROSS, L. 1975, *Ethnc Identity*. Palo Alto, Calif.: Mayfield.

KREJCI, J. and VELIMSKY, V. 1981, *Ethnic and Political Nations in Europe*. London: Croom Helm.

LEMAN, J. 1987, *From Challenging Culture to Challenged Culture*. Leuven: Leuven University Press.

LE PAGE, R.B. and TABOURET-KELLER, A. 1985, *Acts of Identity*. Cambridge: C.U.P.

6 Linguistic Correction and Semantic Skills in the Spanish Children

JOSÉ A. FERNÁNDEZ DE ROTA Y MONTER and MARIA DEL PILAR IRIMIA FERNÁNDEZ

The project discussed here concerns approximately 50 children of Spanish immigrants. These children were admitted between the last year of kindergarten and the fifth year of primary school in one of the most highly rated Dutch-language schools in Brussels. This school, the St.-Jan Berchmans college, primarily attracts Flemish pupils from outside its immediate vicinity. Parents send their children there because of the excellent reputation the school enjoys. The Spanish children come predominantly from the surrounding working-class neighbourhood, which is inhabited largely by Spanish and Moroccan immigrants. In general terms, the Spanish pupils can be considered as belonging to the so-called second generation of immigrants. In other words, they were born in Brussels. Most of these families have a rural background. Geographically, most are from the north of Spain, the majority from Asturias and the rest from Galicia and Leon. Generally, the parents are unskilled workers.

The Formulation of the Problem

The point of departure for this article is constituted by the data assembled during an evaluation week in Brussels. Of course, our contact, although intense, was obviously only an initial approach. Consequently, our considerations must be understood basically as suggestions or questions rather than as categorical statements. Our evaluation of the level of

acquisition of linguistic skills in Spanish rests on a series of tests of 'Evaluation of Minimal Education' developed by the Service for Evaluation and Renewal in Education of the Spanish Ministry of National Education. These tests had already been used with various Spanish communities in Spain in the beginning and middle cycles of primary education. The two cycles contain age groups that correspond to the 2nd and 5th grades, respectively, of Belgian primary education.

Our formulation of the problem proceeded from the need to make a comparison in one way or another between the Spanish pupils of the Foyer Project and their contemporaries in Spain. Because of the limited number of Spanish pupils per grade in the school involved, it was obvious that the statistical data we could compile could only have an indicative value to the extent that our study would attempt to place them in their context and in the framework of mainly qualitative analyses. Moreover, the clear disproportion in opportunities between the trilingual pupils in Brussels and monolingual children in Spain required the introduction of special variants for the pupils of our samples selected in Spain.

With these considerations in mind, we decided to apply the same series of tests in a school with pupils from a rural municipality whose predominant mother tongue in their everyday conversation is Galician[1], and in a school in a suburb of La Coruña with pupils whose parents were from the middle class with a predominantly Castillian-speaking surrounding. Both groups (from the 2nd and the 5th grades) of the latter school were considered by their teachers to be normal achievers. In the rural school, however, while the 2nd grade was considered normal for this school, this was not the case for the 5th grade, which was considered problematical and had an achievement level below the norm.

By administering the tests in the two schools, we obtained a twofold contrast for orientation. The rural school with its problems of bilinguality could have been the school of the Project pupils if their parents had not emigrated to Brussels. The urban school would probably be the kind of school the Project pupils would go to if their parents were to return soon to Spain. Moreover, our qualitative and context interest gained in nuances. The various difficulties of bilinguality or quasi-monolinguality of these schools and the cultural characteristics of both of the environments, with which we were quite familiar, provided us with the opportunity to make valuable findings in our comparative study.

In addition, our research in Brussels, within the limitations of the short duration of our stay, involved a number of typically anthropological concerns. Thus, we examined not only linguistic skills but also cultural implications, feelings of identity, levels of social integration in the class, and the complex play of the various perspectives of the experiment: parents of the Spanish pupils, Flemish and Spanish teachers, the Spanish pupils themselves, and so on.

The Linguistic Research

Our discussion of the results of the linguistic skills tests, which we include here in an appendix, will first stress the varying proportions in the results between the three schools in different concrete respects. While the global results initially confirmed the expected hierarchy, with the urban school of La Coruña on top, then the rural school, and finally the Brussels pupils, this hierarchy is characterised not only by different levels of attainment but also by significant changes in the sequence of learning for certain items. Obviously, not only the difficulties of multilinguality and the cultural environment influence all of this, but the didactic methodology and even the different criteria of the curriculum of Spain and Belgium have an effect. Thus, for example, the Spanish schools begin to teach reading and writing already in the last year of kindergarten, while this is only done in the 1st grade in Belgium. Moreover, we have to keep in mind that our trilingual pupils in Brussels learn to read and write in Spanish and Dutch, while reading and writing in French— the language that is best mastered on the oral level among them—begins only in the 3rd grade. After these considerations, we shall discuss the most significant results.

First and foremost, we can refer to a series of items whereby the difference between monolinguality and multilinguality is not supposed to be a handicap; for example, in handwriting. In this item of the beginning cycle, the results reverse the hierarchical order indicated above: the pupils in Brussels obtain here the best results, followed immediately by the rural pupils, and finally the pupils from La Coruña. In the drafting of letters, an item of the second cycle, the urban pupils (Brussels and La Coruña) obtained the same results, which were much better than those of the pupils of the rural school. As regards study techniques for this same cycle, no pupil from Brussels or from the rural school passed this test, while a significant minority from La Coruña did pass. Still for this same cycle, no pupil from Brussels[2] or from the rural school passed the test on the application of categories of parsing (subject-predicate), while the La Coruña pupils obtained good results. Even more remarkable are the results of the item that asked the pupils to use a dictionary: the Brussels children scored low and the rural children somewhat lower still. All of this is probably due to the concrete orientations of teaching in each school. With regard to the test of parsing, if it were not an exception, it would be important to ask how the teaching is conducted on these logico-formal linguistic levels, which, since it is common to the various languages they study, could serve as a link for mental integration if they are drafted by the teachers working as a team.

Moving on to the theme of reading, we find ourselves among the items whereby the differences of bi- or trilinguality could emerge very clearly. And, indeed, the Brussels pupils have considerable difficulty in reading speed and in the type of reading, their results for both cycles being lower than those of the rural pupils, and clearly lower than those of the La Coruña pupils. The pronunciation of one of the Brussels pupils is typically that of a foreigner, and the others also have a strong contamination in pronunciation and intonation. In reading comprehension, the level of the Brussels children is again clearly lower in both grades. None of the Brussels pupils, neither in the beginning nor in the middle cycle, passed the composition test asking the pupils to tell something in a coherent text. Oral expression was not tested statistically, but the Project pupils obviously had to contend with substantial lexical difficulties and helped each other with French to explain many words.

The results clearly take another turn when we consider oral comprehension of Spanish for both levels (in the second cycle this corresponds to the item 'comprehension and recall of a story'). The results of the Brussels pupils approach those of the Castillian speakers from La Coruña. The Galician speakers had the most difficulties in these areas.

When we examine our results as a whole and distinguish between the beginning and middle cycle, we note a striking difference between the Brussels school and the rural school in the beginning cycle and a relatively small difference between the rural school and the La Coruña school. In the middle cycle, however, the results of the rural pupils, taken as a whole, are slightly lower than those of the Brussels pupils. We have already noted that the class chosen from this rural school had a lower achievement level than what was considered normal for this school.

To draw up a balance of the above, we would have to stress the important individual differences between the pupils of the Foyer experiment. As regards their level of acquisition of Spanish, there are certainly various special circumstances, each of which contributes to the balance, such as the fact that the parents may or may not always speak Spanish at home as well as the frequency and duration of the visits the pupils make to Spain. Of course, in both cases, the degree of purity of Spanish linguistic usage and, more generally, the cultural level of the family environment have an influence. All of this could be more critical than the advantage of the large number of class hours in Spanish during the first two years of primary school offered by the Project, which does not alter the fact that this does provide valuable assistance as regards linguistic skills and, particularly, cultural integration. In comparison with the pupils from Spain, they are clearly under the level of the pupils from La Coruña. To obtain a comparable set of statistics, one must turn to a rural area with major linguistic and cultural difficulties and, within that area, to a group that is recognised as being under the normal level. Let us keep in mind that, even in this case, it was the items that were not directly related to the ability to use Spanish *correctly* that led to this result, together with the already cited fact that oral expression, which would probably manifest a great difference, was not statistically measured. In spite of great efforts to reduce the distance, the pupils of the Project are seen as foreigners, who, in many cases, have achieved good mastery of Spanish.

Oral Comprehension and Expression

On the basis of this general discussion of the items, we consider it essential for our purpose to consider the contrast between the results of oral comprehension and expression of the tested pupils. It is most certainly significant that the Brussels pupils, in spite of their great difficulties in the mastery of spoken and written linguistic codes, achieved a relatively high result in understanding oral Spanish. Perhaps the great effort these pupils make to understand, through the two moderately mastered languages and the later effort to learn a third language, enabled them to obtain high scores in communication with a minimum of linguistic skills. Obviously, our evaluation of their expressive capabilities was not focused—as is customary in this kind of evaluation study—on their skill to transmit meaning content efficiently, but rather on the *correctness* of the use of linguistic codes in oral expression. Of course, since both oral comprehension and oral expression are involved here, the evaluation analysis is highly affected by the virtuosity in the *correct* use of the official linguistic codes. In the evaluation of oral comprehension, however, the linguistic purity of the evaluator is involved and thus the communication receptivity of the pupil dominates the measurement. Linguistic purity as such is thus only secondary.

In order to orient ourselves within this distinction between *communication ability* and *correctness* in the use of linguistic *codes*, it is useful to apply the distinction made by Oksaar (1984) between *rational* and *normative* models. In the *normative model*, the speaker is in a situation in which he has to obey the official normative rules as much as possible. In the *rational model*, however, which is used in the interaction between intimate friends, the speaker strives to achieve as much correctness as possible in the transferred meaning and its possible interpretation by selecting elements and structures without strictly maintaining the official linguistic norms. The listener and theme adapt to the requirements of the situation.

Our extended discussions with small groups of pupils in an open and relaxed atmosphere were always excellent examples of the *rational model* in a frontier situation. By continually jumping from one code to another and by thus introducing very many 'linguistic impurities', accurate communication of meaning was obtained, usually slowly but still efficiently.

The comparison with the bilingual Galician pupils provides nuances for the understanding of this problem. Undoubtedly, the situation of the Galician differs both linguistically and culturally from that of the Brussels pupils. The bilinguality of the Galicians occurs between two Romance languages that are closely related to each other and have co-existed for centuries. The Belgian situation rests on three languages that are much farther from each other and where the signs of plural co-existence in the family and the neighbourhood have a great deal of cyclic improvisation about them. For the former, there is an overlapping of their Galician dialect, which is primarily spoken and domestic, and their expressive *rational model*—a model that can manifest minor variants depending on whether one is speaking with one's classmates or with the older generation, both at home or in the neighbourhood. Since Castillian is traditionally the language of culture and the language used in official documents, the dialectical variant of the local Galician is primarily an oral form that is used at home or in the neighbourhood with intimate friends. In any case, their *rational models* move in the almost established framework of traditional codes in which the official Castillian penetrates in one way or another. The situation of the Belgian pupils with three clearly distinguished normative languages, two of which are primary sources of their *rational models* in the daily speech with the third being imposed in school, places them in a situation of laborious comprehension and expression that is obviously much greater and where the potential ambiguity of phonetically distinct but semantically similar words is a constant challenge in the striving for as much precision and distinction as possible.

A nine-year-old pupil of the Foyer experiment told us how she always spoke Dutch at school, always French at home with her brothers and sisters, but mostly Spanish and sometimes French with her parents and Galician and French with her aunt. Undoubtedly, each of these languages in the various conversations is strongly contaminated with the other languages used by the speaker. The problem expands when we leave the home situation of the pupils. Thus, for example, the French of their Spanish neighbours or of the Spanish Dutch speakers at school, the French of their Italian or Moroccan neighbours, the French of their Flemish peers, and so on constitute an endless complex of variants and gradations in microdialectal shades. They cannot call upon a rational model that rests on specific customary or stereotypical bases, but their models must necessarily and very obviously differ in the diverse and complex linguistic situations. Even in their conversation with friends or family, they are often obliged to make their linguistic expression and understanding dynamic and flexible in a creative way.

The counterpole of the situation we have sketched would be represented by the everyday conversation between the members of the same linguistic community. When the same standard sentences are repeated without anything especially new having to be said, we receive the impression that the language speaks through the persons. Under such circumstances, conversational partners use[3] habitual sentences from their common language and seem to limit themselves to choosing between options that are offered by their linguistic heritage stored in the memory. What is more, their common cultural experience permits them large margins of similarity in their personal meaning frameworks. In no sense do we wish to minimise the value of this everyday speech, which is not always so contentless as it may seem and in which the people feel themselves to be identical to themselves, since they live in conditions that are identical to previous conditions and they employ an always statically identical language in moments of magic imperishability. The only thing we wish to do is draw attention to the characteristics of a type of language in which the language is employed within an extremely strict normative framework and where the propositional content of the sentence can shine in great clarity.

It is true that this kind of stereotyped sentence is clearly used by the Brussels pupils to whom we refer. These everyday repetitions, which bring a certain calm to the linguistic anxiety, often turn up within the family or in conversations with their most intimate friends. The complex context in which they are situated and to which we have referred, however, often and in very distinct situations prevents this kind of routine from obtaining the expected efficiency. The sentences most used by them will all too often not be understood, and in order to be understood they have to call upon other phrases and words to replace others in the same sentences, use long circumlocutions that they think express the same thing, and, finally, search for similarities that make communication possible. The analogies do not always work, and are so far-fetched that they create confusion instead. Those present will then discuss the degree to which a similarity exists or not. One will sometimes have to change one's own linguistic convictions or expand the known meaning of some words.

In the sketched situations, if the language can be a source of mis-understanding, the conversation can lead to more dialogue in the need or the effort to make oneself understood. And the fact of speaking more about facts and actions can offer extended occasions to negotiations and re-ordering of meaning contents. From this, one can become more conscious of everything language means by making oneself understandable and by understanding oneself what is said. In this language—Steiner (1980) describes translation as a kind of linguistic usage '*in extremis*'—it no longer seems that the language speaks through the people. Our main characters change, in a certain sense, into masters of the language.

The Integration

Hitherto, we have tried to present a few important implications that are proper to cases of plural linguistic complexity as we have studied them. To clarify our objective, a distinction can be made between various levels to which we shall refer when we speak of language on the basis of differing situations and interests. Thus, for example, the language can be bent to become a cultural classification label. It is precisely in the complex environment of differing identities and ethnic groups in which these children live that the various languages will serve as the most characteristic distinguishing element for each group. It is the most striking empirical element around which the characteristics of an identification stereotype cluster.

On another level, we can look at language as a complex of already acquired or still to be acquired skills. Here, the languages can be studied at the level of codes and their meaning possibilities from a semiotic point of view. Grammarians and philologists have generally concentrated on the formal characteristics of the language. Often, they have considered this level of analysis to be the language in itself. Its importance for teaching a language— the mother tongue or a foreign language—is clear and has an all-encompassing effect.

In addition to these two levels, which are easy to distinguish and lend themselves to formal study, there is a complex overlayer that is controlled by attention to discourse, to human language converted into action, into social and cultural interplay. This is a layer in which meaning, conceived as the content of life experience, is central. Here, language is primarily dialogue or attempts at dialogue, understanding or not understanding, and the dynamics of communication. In this overlayer, the two previous levels are present as well as the influence of social and economic structures, diverse motivations, friendship and enmity, the cohesion of the group to which one belongs or refers, and so on. Attention to the importance of this last layer—to which the anthropologist must be very sensitive (Geertz, 1973 and 1983; Parkin, 1982;

Lison Tolosana, 1983; Fernández de Rota, 1988)—as well as the considerations sketched in the last section on the concept of the *rational model* acquire here a special coherence.

In this way, if we consider not only the integration of these pupils in their basic environment, at home and in the neighbourhood, but also their integration in the world of the school that is structured as a function of educational concerns, we are confronted with critical questions. Up to what point do the upper communication levels function efficiently in the school? Are the Spanish pupils and the experiment their group represents well integrated in the school as a whole? These questions were first approached by working out two sociograms per class. One of them examines the preferences of spontaneous socialising by means of a question concerning with which two classmates the pupil would choose to go for a trip. The Spanish pupils, who formed a minority, clearly chose to group together when there were sufficient Spanish pupils of the same sex to provide a minimum of autonomy. Nevertheless, they seldom formed groups that one could consider isolated. In the classes in which there were too few Spanish pupils of the same sex, they apparently had no difficulties in joining one or another group of Belgian children. The contrast, however, is very large when we examine the sociograms for which the question of the preference for study partners was asked. Since most of the courses were taught in Dutch, the Spanish pupils sought out Flemish pupils as semantic advisers. Many of these Flemish pupils, since they were used to studying together with the Spanish pupils, responded to this choice by reciprocal preference. In this way, the groups of Spaniards appeared to be much more integrated in this sociogram. We did not ask the concrete question of with whom they would prefer to study French. But since the Spanish pupils know this language better than the Flemish pupils, the comments of the teachers indicated that the Flemish pupils often seek the Spanish pupils to serve as semantic advisers.

The study relations are undoubtedly more precise and formalised and originate not so much in friendship relations, as reflected in the sociograms on the preferences for a companion for a trip. It is self-evident that there are factors that could hinder the formation of friendships, such as varying linguistic skills, differences in socio-economic status, and the fact of having formed a separate group for a number of hours during the first years of school. However, the need to learn a language and the support that is desirable from those who have a better mastery of the language seems to be a valuable instrument for promoting mutual approaches. That is to say, the difficulties that flow from the differing linguistic skills can, in specific conditions, be an important stimulus and promoter of human relations that facilitate the communication between the individuals of different groups.

Furthermore, just as significant is the fact that usually the Flemish teachers, who were closely involved with the Spanish pupils in the first years, were very well liked by them. It is true that these were teachers who voluntarily accepted this task and, consequently, were highly motivated. Nevertheless, it seems that their special linking position with the Flemish ethnic group and their position as principal linguistic advisers for Dutch placed them in a very positive communication position. Once again, the different linguistic skills were here more of a stimulus for unification than for division.

With the attention we have devoted to these two circumstances, we do not want to give the impression that the course of our analysis deviates from the largely linguistic theme we are trying to present. The social circumstances that condition these integration relationships are multiple, and we only want to stress the possible specific weight that linguistic aspects occupy in them. Indeed, our linguistic orientation ascribes a central role to the richness of communication.

By attending to this theme and by the elementary distinction between linguistic levels that we have proposed, we tried to avoid the danger of conceiving language as that which is studied by grammarians and linguists. Undoubtedly, there are ever more linguists who are far removed from this danger, but for a very long time it was thought that the abstraction level on which they work is not only a methodical approach to language but that it is the language in its full reality. We understand by this that the dynamic reality of the language evolves between the complex of linguistic skills and meaning restrictions that are preserved in the memory and the concrete expressive act of each moment. This act always involves a certain change of the mnemonic inheritance. (See Ricoeur (1980) and Benveniste (1977).) The theories of speech act (Austin, 1962; Searle, 1969) also approach this way of thinking. The former point of view is all the more dangerous in education where one or more languages are studied in specific courses. Of course, the effort to have the pupils acquire concrete skills that enable them to use a certain language correctly is extraordinarily difficult and important.

It is not our intention to cast doubt on all of this, but it can be beneficial to realise that our series of linguistic tests, which are situated within the customary co-ordinates of what is understood by language evaluation, were only capable of astonishing the attentive evaluator with the high level of oral comprehension. It is precisely in a relatively extreme case like that of the Spanish children of the Project that attention to the different levels on which language can be observed appears to be all the more necessary. It is obvious that our tests measured only a small portion of the linguistic domain, and it is precisely that part in which the excellent polyglots failed the most. What results could we have obtained if our study had tried to measure their capability of providing creative responses to a particular linguistic difficulty of expression or comprehension? Our study was not geared to this nor was it geared to the measurement of the ability to consider language in itself or the ability to comprehend or express a great deal with few resources. It could be that an evaluation of these linguistic aspects would have yielded very different results.

On 'Belgians' and 'Moroccans'

Our situation during the time we spent at the St.-Jan Berchmanscollege was certainly totally different from the situation a teacher could have who taught a course for an entire school year. In our situation, we could use our time to listen, to understand, to learn and to evaluate since we were not obliged to teach. Therefore, and also because of the unusualness of our presence, our dialogue with the pupils yielded an entire series of questions and suggestions.

In the line of these considerations, it is important to understand that, while the situation of these pupils requires from them a certain level of linguistic creativity, this creativity is no less necessary for those who try to understand them, be it their teachers, their usual semantic advisers, their classmates or their evaluators.

We, too, expanded our analogy fields in our contact with them, and we, too, discovered new possible meanings. Concern with this kind of creative skill that establishes comprehension has been the fundamental axis of hermeneutic thought of recent years (e.g. Gadamer, 1977; Ricoeur, 1969, 1980).

In our short stay, we obviously could not observe in detail the didactic attitudes and methods of the teachers of the school. The popularity of the Flemish teachers who worked with the Spanish pupils as well as the popularity of others of their colleagues, however, allows us to presume the enormous effort made to attain creative linguistic comprehension. We shall cite a few examples from our dialogues with the children and try to derive some useful suggestions from them.

After we had spoken with them and had attentively listened to the tape-recorded conversations, we tried to discern a few 'key words' (Evans-Pritchard, 1980) on the basis of our anthropological orientation: words loaded with a rich multiplicity of meanings, rich in connotations and that perhaps form the semantic axis of their cultural system. Turner (1974, 1980) has proposed a similar concept of 'root symbols'. Of course, the conversations were initially guided, but all in all we were obliged in the dialogues by the spontaneity and initiative of the children to devote attention to themes we had not initially foreseen. Thus, one of the words that was the richest in meaning for them was the word '*belga*' (Belgian).

As we have already noted, the collective feeling of identity was for them primarily linked to the use of a language. Probably linked to this is also the idea of a territory from which one originated, but the language that is spoken at home and its contaminations in French are the primary and most pronounced empirical element for identifying an identity group. In this way, they ordinarily call the Walloons the '*franceses*' (French) and distinguish them from the '*flamanes*' (Flemish). The correct term in Spanish is *flamenco*. The term *flamán*, which is always used by the pupils and their parents, is an obvious contamination of the French. With the term *belga*, they mean either the Walloons or the European residents of Brussels, Belgians and otherwise, but all the more so if they are born in Brussels. So we heard that certain children were 'not Moroccans but Belgians like us'. To the question of whether there were many Belgians in the school, some answered: 'Yes, we are Belgians.' Others, however, would deny this, after which a discussion would begin to clarify the situation, which clearly indicated the ambiguity of identification this term generates. In another conversation, a girl told us how a Flemish classmate in an argument told her that the Spaniards did not belong in this country or in this school but that they should go back to their own country. To this, the girl had replied: 'You don't belong here either. You *flamanes* are from another country. This school is for Spaniards.' With this new use of the term, *belga* is applicable to all white French speakers who are born there, and she, as a French speaker born in Brussels, could consider herself in this respect as a Belgian, a specific subtype of Belgians, namely a child of Spanish immigrants.

From this point of view, derived from the life in their neighbourhoods, the term 'Belgian' does not apply very clearly to the '*flamanes*'. In the function of their language, which is different from that of the majority in Brussels, the Flemish are seen as aliens in their own country. The children themselves, however, in spite of their convincingly proclaimed Spanishness, are, in contrast with the '*marroquinos*', the Europeans of Brussels and hence the Belgians in their neighbourhoods. And in contrast to the Flemish, they are the ones who speak the French that is spoken on the street, their usual French. So this is one more reason they can call themselves Belgians. While the girl replied to her Flemish classmate from the viewpoint of the logic of her neighbourhood, the situation of the Spanish children in the school is different in reality. Thus, one of the most critical of the pupils told us that 'they make you feel like an alien in this school'. That is to say, in the school Dutch is the official, obligatory and dominant language and is the mother tongue of the Belgian majority of the school. With respect to the school, he was the alien with his

French and his neighbourhood. In contrast with the ethnic confusion of his complex neighbourhood in which he could sometimes feel more Spanish, particularly at home, and sometimes more Belgian, particularly on the street, at school he was classified in a dichotomous way as a Spaniard with respect to the Belgians: they made him 'feel like an alien'. At school, finally, the Flemish pupils are more *Belgian* than they are.

This brief analysis clearly shows how the term 'Belgian' is here clad with a range of meanings and ambiguity and that allows us to presume an entire network of connotations that could be examined in detail. What is the attitude of a teacher who listens to such a set of comments and discussions? A possible and rapidly clarifying answer could be that both the Flemings and the Walloons are Belgians and that those who are not registered officially as having Belgian nationality are not Belgians, even though they might have been born in Brussels. Here the teacher could show his or her astonishment at the ignorance of the pupils. All of this would be correct and justified, but we are of the opinion that the teacher would then have only imposed a crude geographical map without a geographical heart in opposition to the vital profundity and wealth of emotional connotations of the term 'Belgian' for the pupils.

However, if the teacher is gifted with profound communicative comprehension and is capable of expanding the term 'Belgian' with semantic creativity and making it broader than what it means for himself or herself, then the conversation with the pupils can be the occasion for an unforgettable lesson in linguistics. Geography would be transformed into a deep, vital reality for the pupils.

Obviously, the 'error' of the pupil is not comparable to that of a person who lives in a distant country and does not know that Flemings and Walloons live in Belgium. Such ignorance would be an error in the geographical knowledge of this person, a lack of cultural knowledge on a theme that is far beyond his own life experience. For the Spanish girl in Brussels, however, this error rests on her human experience. It concerns the cognitive geography of her home, of her neighbourhood, and her school. It is very obvious that not everybody who lives in a particular country would feel related to it and also that many people and entire regions experience a disturbing ambiguity of identification. The teacher can universalise the personal experience of his or her pupil and cite the problems of the people of Ulster, Lebanon or the Basque region, the generation problems of the immigrants, and their own Flemish problem as problems that can be understood and experienced with very different meaning contents depending on the point of view. Their geography lesson would then become an inspired lesson in semantic geography.

Naturally, the environmental geography of their neighbourhood involves many other groups and probably analysis of the terms *marroquinos* and *moros* is of no less didactic importance. In Spanish, the terms *marroquíes* and *moros* are used. The former is the cultural and polite term, the latter a popular term with the connotations noted below in the text. (*Marroquino* is also a contamination of the French.) The meanings of these two terms undoubtedly differ and intersect. For a Spaniard from the rural Northwest of Spain, the Moors are the enemies against whom their parents and grandparents fought in the African war. It is also a representative term for all non-Christians and, metaphorically, for any one who speaks an unknown language. Finally, the Moors are legendary, prehistorical people, the original inhabitants of the earth, the builders of prehistorical monuments, those who left behind mysterious treasures of gold, the protagonists of all the legendary battles against evil. As the mother of one of these pupils said: 'I have heard many people talk about the Moors, but before I came here I never saw any.' Here, however, they are people with whom they share the neighbourhood or even a house, the people with whom the men work, and sometimes the playmates of their children.

When the children talk about the *marroquinos*, they generally present a negative image. Some, however, do not agree with this and consider it racist. They talk about their strange customs, like their way of praying, their fasting during Ramadan, and their slaughtering of sheep even in their apartments. But, during their summer vacations in Spain, confusion arises with other terms. Thus, one child who went to Mallorca heard his father say that the people there speak 'like the Moors'. The logic of this statement seems very clear to the pupils, who confirm the great similarity between the terms *mallorquino* and *marroquino* and for whom it is thus certain that the *mallorquinos* speak *marroquino* (Moroccan). Another pupil told us that his grandfather in Asturia, the home region of his parents, told him that Galicians are like Moors because of their way of speaking.

The teachers could certainly spend some time on the confusion whereby similar terms are used to create stereotypes in different stories. But here, too, the semantic analysis of the content these terms have for them and their families can be expanded by an evocation of history and be compared with the meaning equivalent terms have for their Belgian classmates in Dutch.

Other terms can be considered similarly by way of examples. The term *grandfather*, for example, evokes its full meaning for the Spanish immigrant child who returns to the house of the birth of his parents in the summer. It has a profound cultural echo of the old *patrucio*, the head of the house and the domestic descent group of Northwest Spain. Terms that express a value judgement, like neatness and riches, turned out to be enormously suggestive, whereby a comparative method was used in conjunction with their own experience.

There are perhaps few terms so critical for these children as the term *neighbourhood*. This is certainly their real, prosaic and complex fatherland. We are of the opinion that one of the pillars for their potential cultural integration can be found in the neighbourhood. Perhaps the semantic and sociological analysis of their neighbourhood and its parts, the being able to understand and love their neighbourhood, is one of the fundamental challenges in the search for their own identity.

Masters of the Language

In our study, we started from an interpretation of the linguistic skills in Spanish of the Spanish pupils. We have pointed out their limitations and the didactic efforts to reduce them as a theme that is certainly of great importance. Our interest, however, was focused on gauging, by following the trail of their deepest linguistic skills, their capacity for extensive communication with rather limited resources. We have tried to emphasise that the linguistic education—and, in a special way, the extreme circumstances such as those we studied—must be very sensitive to the perception and evaluation of the linguistic skill of the pupil and must be aware that the *creative* understanding of the teacher can be a decisive factor in the success of the experiment.

There is no doubt that attention to semantics, if we remain with the traditional focus of anthropology, is an essential element in this educational experiment for the intercultural comprehension and the integration of distinct interests and standpoints. The anthropological use we refer to customarily cites between quotation marks textual sentences of its informers exactly as they are stated. In this way, before they are evaluated or estimated for value, they are established in a text, like a text that one must try to place in its context, to analyse, and assign weight for its cultural content. Only then does one usually bring forth *key words* that are loaded with a special wealth of meaning. Even though they belong to the language in which the anthropologist writes, they must be written in italics. They are mysterious words that mean much more than the anthropologist can initially presume. They are words that distinguish themselves and, therefore, must be written in another letter type. The secret of semantic study that we would advocate here consists of being able to identify and understand these words and to build a lesson around them for everyone. If one proceeds in this way, then both the researcher and the researched, both the teacher and the pupil, are enriched with doubt about the value of ambiguity, and they become more creative in the search for analogies.

The experiment that we studied is based on a surrounding world in which the multiplicity of languages, which embody different stereotypes, sets the boundaries between the various ethnic groups. In its pedagogical activity, it tries to instil linguistic skills, but we think that if one looks further than these two levels, which are concerned with the linguistic activity and the content of meaning, these same boundaries can become precisely a challenge for the search for ties that unite.

With a feeling for anthropology, the experiment is transformed into a great ambition: the strong desire to be no longer slaves but masters of the language. We as teachers always stress *linguistic purity* as something unquestionably necessary, but let us not forget, at some moments of our lives, that *linguistic impurity* can be very rich.

Notes

1. To date most of our work of collecting anthropological data has been centred on this rural district. There have been a number of publications on the subject.

2. We do not really know what this result is due to. If this were not an exception, it would be essential to work out how the didactic element will function at these logical-formal levels of the language. As these are common to the different languages being studied, they could be used as a link for mental integration if programmed by the team of teachers concerned.

3. In certain linguistic schools, concrete speech has been thought of as the *use* of specific linguistic skills. We are of the opinion here that the common and stereotyped sentences can approach this idea of *use*. Normally, we do not limit ourselves to just making use of our skills, as though our memories were closets in which we hang up or take out our linguistic jackets as and when needed. Nor do we limit ourselves to the mere updating of our linguistic options but we make use of our linguistic and cultural skills to produce creative language.

References

AUSTIN, J.L. 1962, *How to do Things with Words*. Oxford: Clarendon Press.
BENVENISTE, E. 1977, *Problemas de lingüística general II*. México: Siglo XXI. (Orig. 1974).
EVANS-PRITCHARD, E. 1980, *La religión nuer*. Madrid: Taurus. (Orig. 1956)

FERNÁNDEZ DE ROTA MONTER, J.A. 1988, *Antropología Social y Semántica*. In C. LISON TOLOSANA (Ed) *Antropología Social sin fronteras* 55–109. Madrid: Instituto de Sociología Aplicada.

GADAMER, H.G. 1977, *Verdad y método*. Salamanca: Sígueme. (Orig. 1975).

GEERTZ, C. 1973, *The Interpretation of Cultures*. London: Hutchinson.

—— 1983, *Local Knowledge*. New York: Basic Books Inc.

LISON TOLOSANA, C. 1983, *Antropología Social y Hermenéutica*. Madrid: Fondo de Cultura Económica.

OKSAAR, E. 1984, Multilingüismo y multiculturalismo desde el punto de vista del lingüista. In T. HUSEN and S. OPPER (eds), *Educación multicultural y multilingüe*. 73–60. Madrid: Narcea.

PARKIN, D. (ed.) 1982, *Semantic Anthropology*. London: Academic Press Inc.

RICOEUR, P. 1969, *Le conflit des interprétations*. Paris: Ed. du Seuil.

—— 1980, *La metáfora viva*. Madrid: Europa. (Orig. 1975).

SEARLE, J.D. 1969 *Speech Acts*. Cambridge: Cambridge University Press.

STEINER, G. 1980, *Después de Babel. Aspectos del lenguaje y la traducción*. Madrid: Fondo de Cultura Económica. (Orig. 1975).

TURNER, V. 1974, *Dramas, Fields and Metaphors*. Ithaca: Cornell University Press.

—— 1980 *La selva de los símbolos*. Madrid: Siglo XXI. (Orig. 1967).

Appendix
Results of the Tests of 'Minimum Levels of Learning' in Spanish Language.

FIRST LEVEL (8 years old) (1)

ITEMS	BRUSSELS Pass	BRUSSELS No pass	RURAL MUNICIPALITY Pass	RURAL MUNICIPALITY No pass	LA CORUÑA Pass	LA CORUÑA No pass
ORAL COMPREHENSION						
1. Read a sequence	5	1	16	10	14	5
2. Spatial	4	2	17	9	14	5
3. Cause–effect	3	3	15	11	15	4
TOTAL	12	6	48	30	43	14
READING COMPREHENSION						
4. Lexical inscription	1	5	18	8	11	8
5. Global text	1	5	15	11	12	7
6. Synthesis	2	4	12	14	7	12
7. Attention to one issue	2	4	11	15	10	9
8. Detection of truth	0	6	4	22	7	12
9. Detection of falsity	3	3	24	2	13	6
10. Content	1	5	11	15	8	11
TOTAL	10	32	95	87	68	65
ORTHOGRAPHICAL RULES						
11. "N" and "M"	3	3	18	8	16	3
HANDWRITING						
12.	5	1	21	5	13	6
SPATIO-GRAPHICAL ORIENTATION						
13.	1	5	7	19	12	7
ORTHOGRAPHY						
14. Usual words: % errors per words	10.53%		8.59%		7.22%	
TEXT						
15. Structure of the text in sentences	0	6	14	12	8	11
TOTAL OF ALL THE ITEMS	31	57	203	161	160	106

FIRST LEVEL (2)

ITEMS	BRUSSELS	RURAL MUNICIPALITY	LA CORUÑA
READING SPEED	43	55.6	81.3
TYPE OF READING			
1. Syllabic	2	0	0
2. Hesitant	1	5	3
3. Normal	3	5	7
COMPREHENSIVE READING			
Number of incorrect answers:			
0	3	4	9
1	0	4	0
2	1	2	0
3	2	0	1
ERRORS IN INTONATION			
0	2	6	8
1	1	4	2
2	2	0	0
3	1	0	0
ERRORS IN PAUSE			
0	1	5	3
1	2	3	2
2	1	1	2
3	0	1	3
4	1	0	0
5 or more	1	0	0

SECOND LEVEL (11 years old)

ITEMS	BRUSSELS		RURAL MUNICIPALITY		LA CORUÑA	
	Pass	No pass	Pass	No pass	Pass	No pass
Understand and recall an oral story	4	2	11	13	16	4
Apply concepts of subject-predicate	0	6	0	24	15	5
Letter writing	3	3	1	23	10	10
Cleanliness, order, handwriting	4	2	8	16	14	6
Use of dictionary	1	5	3	21	6	14
Reading comprehension	2	4	9	15	16	4
Written story telling	0	6	5	19	16	4
Orthography	1	5	5	19	12	8
Study techniques	0	6	0	24	5	15
Reading level	2	4	5	3	10	0
Reading speed	79.5		99.8		149.5	
	Pass	No pass	Pass	No pass	Pass	No pass
TOTAL	17	43	47	157	122	88

7 Language and the Teaching of Mathematics to Turkish Children

KATHLEEN SNOECK

Introduction

Mathematics has always had a privileged position in Western culture. It established its place in the school curriculum in the nineteenth century and ever since it has been one of the major components in every education programme. In recent decades, owing to the great impact of technology, its importance has even increased and nowadays it is used as a major social and educational tool for selection and stratification.

How the learning of mathematics is influenced by different variables has received a lot of attention lately. Mathematics is viewed less and less as a universal, fixed body of knowledge, beyond the boundaries of space and time. A number of studies (e.g. Wilder, 1981) approach mathematics through the history of mathematical ideas and concepts and their links to cultural and social phenomena. Moreover, cultural and environmental interfaces are accepted as part of the discussion of mathematics education, or as Bishop points out: 'Mathematics education is a form of cultural induction. It concerns values, customs, habits and in general a particular way of viewing the world' (1985: 5).

Currently, owing to the 'Mathematics for All' movement in the 1950s, a growing number of children in the most diverse societies are confronted with mathematics at a very young age. In developing as well as developed countries, the difficulties they face alert us to the complexity of their learning process and the existence of underlying factors by which it is affected. It is claimed that not one but a conglomerate of different (often situational) factors influence their learning and achievement.

115

Learning Mathematics in a Second Language

One of these factors, which is gaining more attention than has formerly been the case, is language. The fact that millions of children are forced to learn mathematics in a second or even a third language led to a revived interest in the role of language in cognitive development and has given rise to considerable research on the acquisition of language and the understanding or teaching of mathematics. Despite all this, important questions regarding the nature of the language of instruction, the importance of the mother tongue and the interaction between second language and mother tongue have not been fully answered yet.

Aside from the difficulties in many developing countries, second-language problems relating to mathematics are most striking for immigrant children. Although it should be acknowledged that sociocultural influences are also at work, language is considered one of the major handicaps with respect to formal education.

Throughout Western Europe ethnic minority children obtain mathematics education in a language different from their own mother tongue. In particular for these children the social relevance of achievement in mathematics is not to be underestimated. Often, failing in maths means failing in school and leads to a lack of opportunities for future career perspectives. Ethnic minority children usually show, compared with their monolingual Belgian classmates, a poor performance in mathematics. From the first year of elementary school, we often witness a progressive retardation.

As mathematics education should be considered as an encounter between cultural background, experience and the cognitive structure of the child with the activities, language and concepts of mathematics, this is not surprising at all. The more the values, activities and language at home deviate from those in the middle-class oriented school curriculum, the more profound difficulties can be expected. Too often we witness a complete breakdown between the child's language and cultural background and the world and language of the school. Therefore most immigrant children come to associate mathematics with frustration and inferiority. Because it is taught without any linkage to the experiences and linguistic knowledge of the child it is generally experienced as something artificial; a subject that has practically nothing to do with the world of the immigrant child and is bound never to be deeply assimilated.

The Turkish Children Within the Foyer Project

Apart from affective considerations, the process of learning mathematics in a foreign language also gives rise to problems on the level of cognition and pedagogy. We shall be mainly focusing on these aspects, pointing out some of the problems observed in having to learn mathematics in a second language. Our comments are based on work with Turkish immigrant children in the first years of elementary school. The children are all part of the Foyer project for bicultural education in the Brussels agglomeration. This Turkish-Flemish project started in 1982 and now 24 children are participating in the first, second and third grades of a Dutch-speaking primary school. Most children began nursery school at the age of three, where they received both Dutch and Turkish language instruction. Before they entered school they had no knowledge of the Dutch language. At home they speak Turkish or a dialect form of it. The majority of the children live in the centre of Old-Molenbeek, a district near the centre of Brussels. Most of the families originate from rural villages in Turkey, such as Konya and Eskisehir. Usually they are poor, residing in old and dilapidated houses. The children grow up in an impoverished and rather isolated environment, with very little encouragement and stimulation from the parents. Unlike the Italian, Spanish and Moroccan children that participate in the other Foyer projects, they hardly speak or understand French despite the fact that this is the dominant language or so-called 'language of the streets' in Brussels. The rather isolated situation of the Turkish community and the sometimes explicit resistance to integration account for this.

In the first year of elementary school the Turkish children spend a lot of time with the Turkish language teacher. He teaches exclusively in Turkish and gives the initial reading and writing lessons. Next to this they also receive Dutch language teaching separately and at the end of the first year they start learning to read and write with the Dutch language teacher. All other content subjects are taught by the primary school teacher, together with the other Belgian children. Owing to practical considerations, mathematics education is received in Dutch with the Dutch-speaking classmates. Therefore special attention should be paid to the relationship between language and the teaching and the learning of mathematics.

Cognitive Skills and Binguality

The literature reveals the need of an adequately developed mother tongue for mathematical thinking. Most scholars stress the role of language in the development of abstract thinking and point out the significance of the abstraction level of the first language for mastering concepts and operation connected with mathematics. Within the Foyer project the importance of learning the Turkish mother tongue is seen as a support, even when learning mathematics in a second language.

Although thinking and language are far from identical and their relationship complex, it is generally accepted that they are closely linked. Language is considered to be a powerful instrument for reasoning and hypothetical thinking, by means of which thought is able to free itself from the immediate context, turning towards abstraction. A deprivation of language capacity can harm this and may have overall negative effects on cognitive development and academic achievement. It is claimed that language cannot be used well for cognitive functioning, unless the child has developed some skill in it. Particularly in mathematics, the observation of learning-processes, the reflection and making explicit of one's thinking and the ability to communicate this, are very important. Children who are not able to do so lack a crucial ingredient for the development of mathematical thinking.

Language also plays a principal role in concept-formation. By means of it we can express and grasp concepts and are able to organise and classify our experiences. A lot of abstract or high-order concepts cannot be conceived without language (Skemp, 1971). Mathematical concepts, too, rely heavily on the application of linguistic categories; for example, with regard to logical connectives, language elements are very important.

If the child cannot use the required linguistic label it will be very hard to express these concepts or to grasp the meaning of reasoning. Children who lack the words are observed to experience difficulties.

Cummins (1979) offers a theoretical framework to explain the relationship between thinking and language in the bilingual child, which has implications that can be drawn for the learning of mathematics. Briefly, Cummins asserts that a beneficial form of bilingualism, or the positive cognitive effects due to the learning of two languages, can only be obtained on the basis of developed first language skills. If education ignores the mother tongue, the risk of semilingualism is high. This means that neither in the home-language, nor the second language, is the child able to function adequately. Then the second language is learned at the expense of the first one, having negative effects on cognitive functioning. In the same vein Cummins argues that first language competence is an important condition for mathematical thinking. Within the Foyer Model this advice is followed by implementation of an extensive mother tongue programme in the first years of primary school.

Another principle in Cummins's theory is connected with the concept of 'linguistic distance', meaning how far two languages are linguistically removed from each other. It is stated that the greater the distance between home language and a foreign language, the more difficult it will be to learn and function in this second language. In the case of mathematics it is often evident that it is not possible to express mathematical relations and concepts in the home language of the child. For example, in some African languages logical connectives are totally absent and cannot be expressed. The differences between Turkish and Dutch are much more subtle. However, it should be pointed out that the remoteness between Turkish and Dutch is more extensive than between Dutch and French, or even Italian.

A specific characteristic for the Turkish language is its use of suffixes. Sentences are mostly constructed by adding words or particles at the end of the major concepts. The verb is mainly placed at the end of a phrase and in the present time the verb 'to be' is omitted, while 'to have' is totally missing. Most nouns are used as class-words and are used without articles with no specification of plurality or singularity. So, for some constructions there is no identical translation in Turkish and *vice-versa*. As an example we take the classical way in which sums are expressed as in '2 and 2 are 4'. Here we have to consider that mathematical symbolism is constructed against the background of European languages. Most of these have a word-order that contains subject–verb–object. Sums also reflect such a word order, placing the verb in the middle of the sentence and not at the end, which might be more self-evident and less artificial for Turkish children.

The Language and the Teaching of Mathematics

Mathematics is taught and learned mainly through the medium of language, which implies that the instruction language of the teacher will play a vital role in the learning process of the child. The understanding of mathematics will be influenced by the understanding of what the teacher says. In this sense Dutch should be acquired at a level which is adequate for instruction and communication. Just as language used by the teacher and in the textbooks may be an impeding factor for monolingual children, this is even more the case for the Turkish children observed. For them Dutch is the school language, rarely used or met outside the classroom. This means that their language competence as compared with Belgian peers is much lower, but they are expected to learn and understand the same as Dutch-speaking children. Teachers have to bear in mind their language limitations and have to overcome the gap between their speech and the capacity of the child to understand. The failure of not being able to bridge this gap can be considered as one of the barriers in the learning of mathematics.

In the mathematics lessons the teacher uses partly ordinary or natural language next to more specific or mathematical speech. For immigrant children the problem is therefore twofold. They have to grasp new mathematical concepts in a new language. This means that two types of understanding have to be present at the same time: academic knowledge (contents of the concepts, skills and ideas) in accordance with socio-cognitive knowledge (the way in which the academic content is presented by the teacher, implying an understanding of the intentions, instructions and explanations) (Osser, 1985).

It is obvious that a lack of appropriate skills for understanding affects the learning process of the child. If an instruction or question is not understood, one cannot expect the child to perform well, even though it might have the capacity to do so. During maths lessons language is constantly used for explaining and verbal labels are applied for improvement of understanding, involving concepts such as 'more', 'less', 'equal' and 'much'. All these words are important tools for understanding mathematics and can impair a more thorough insight into the elementary operations in the first year. Whereas monolingual children come to school with a considerable history of Dutch language acquisition, this is not so for the Turkish children. The Dutch reference frame that supports their understanding is limited, and this demands from the teacher special care and attention. He or she should be aware that the linguistic form in which information and instructions are presented can facilitate or impede the understanding and performance of the child.

Let us compare, for example, the following questions: 'I have 10 fr. and I lose 5 fr. How much do I have left?' and 'How much do I have left if I lose 5 out of 10 fr.?'

Both imply the same operation and contain identical mathematical information. However, the first question is much easier to understand. The 'if . . . then' construction used makes it more complex whereas the short constructions used for the first questions make the intention of the question fairly simple.

In the same way teachers have to make concessions which are important for children who lack the knowledge of the language of education. The more complex the language used by the teacher, the more difficulties children have to face in trying to grasp its content on a linguistic and mathematical level. Some suggestions on how to overcome similar difficulties can be pointed out. In general it is advisable to use simple and short sentences with a minimum of subordinate clauses. Main ideas, important mathematical concepts and keywords should be repeated and given special attention. If they are not relevant, conditional and hypothetical structures should be avoided and active instead of passive constructions should be preferred.

Confusing Concepts

Regarding concept-formation, we have to bear in mind that most mathematical concepts the immigrant children acquire are new words. Therefore they should be introduced with much care with regard to meaning and pronunciation. In Dutch, some elementary concepts, owing to their auditive resemblance, can be difficult to discriminate. As such, the danger of confusion and fuzzy concept-formation is not unlikely when teachers are not aware of this. For example, during exercises on elementary set theory children of the first grade had to classify according to the criteria 'groot' (= Dutch) (big) or 'rood' (= Dutch) (red). For the Turkish children the difference between the words was not perceived, because for them both words sounded exactly the same. As some consonants are hard to differentiate, words such as 'geen' (= Dutch) (no) and 'een' (= Dutch) (one), 'keer' (= Dutch) (time) and 'meer' (= Dutch) (more) are sometimes used without differentiation. Also the confusion between 'meer' (= Dutch) (more) and 'veel' (= Dutch) (much), witnessed with most children of the first year, can be related to this.

In the same way, one word can have different meanings depending on the context in which it is used. In Dutch we say that six is an 'even' (= Dutch) (even) number and at the same time we use 'even' in the construction 'even veel' (= Dutch) (in equal number). As it is observed that immigrant children often use one word instead of two- or three-word expressions (e.g. 'even' instead of 'even veel' or 'zelfde' (= Dutch) (the same) instead of 'hetzelfde aantal als' (= Dutch) (the same number as)) similar examples are hard to make sense of, especially if the necessary metalinguistic knowledge is not present. Another example of this is seen when introducing elementary geometry. Here we are confronted with a family of concepts: 'punt' (= Dutch) (point), 'rechte' (= Dutch) (straight line), 'hoek' (= Dutch) (angle), etc. Many of the concepts used are compound words and semantically very closely related. Again, one word can have different meanings. For example, a 'rechte' is a straight line but when the word is used as an adjective with angle 'rechte hoek' it refers to something else. A 'rechthoek' (= Dutch) (rectangle) on the other hand is a two-dimensional figure, consisting of four 'rechte hoeken' (= Dutch) (right angles). Notice the similarity between 'rechthoek' (rectangle) and 'rechte hoek' (right angle); the words are almost identical and cause confusion for most Turkish children. Owing to their lack of Dutch language capacity compared with monolingual children, it is much harder for them to grasp the full context. So the range of meanings one word or expression might have often remains obscure for them. For these children it is much more difficult to infer from one example or one instance of a concept all other instances. Or as Jones remarks for children who have to learn mathematics in a second language: '[the children] have no chance of grasping the range of meanings they can take in a mathematical setting' (1982: 3).

An equal source of confusion is the variety of ways for saying one thing. Again, this is not as self-evident for the Turkish children as with Dutch-speaking pupils. Take a simple sum such as 3 + 5 = 8. This is only one symbolic representation, but it can be expressed in different ways. In attempting to explain, the teacher can verbalise: 'How much is 3 and 5?', 'I have 3 and I add 5. How much do I have together?', '5 and 3 is ?', 'How much is 5 more than 3?', etc. All these different utterances are in fact full of ambiguities and cause more problems for the Turkish immigrant child.

The Problematic Nature of Modern Mathematics

In Modern Mathematics, too, language problems are sometimes striking. Here we often see a very artificial and specific use of language. Questions are asked: 'Why is this an element of the set A?', 'Why is this not an element?' and the curriculum suggests expressions such as: 'A is the set of blocks equal to yellow'. Here we meet a complex syntax, a specific vocabulary and many symbols which the child must try to make sense of. There is a strong conventional way of representation which demands constant verbal explanation by the teacher. Exercises, in contrast to the conventional sums, look strange and even to adults it is often bewildering to figure out the intention of the instructions. No wonder that many teachers experience difficulties in using modern mathematics with immigrant children. The level of precision and abstraction needed to express and understand modern mathematics is high and causes problems, as these children lack the necessary linguistic experience.

Above all, teachers should be aware of the strong conventional nature of language and presentations. These might look evident for them, but for children, and especially Turkish children, this is not the case. An empty set, for example, has nothing in it, yet we draw lines in it which have a definite number that we are able to count. How can this be? Also, the whole–part relation which dominates modern mathematics is not so evident for immigrant children whose pre-school experiences are not the same as those of a middle-class Belgian child. And here we touch another important point regarding the education of Turkish children.

If there is a danger in ignoring second-language problems, there is also a risk in relating the problems of Turkish children only to language difficulties. If we regard mathematics concept attainment as a mere process of labelling, there is a strong possibility that children will use and acquire concepts without even understanding them. Therefore, when introducing new concepts at least two questions should be asked:

—are there any language difficulties; does the child understand the language of instruction of the teacher and the meaning of the words and conventions used?
—does the child have the necessary experiences to come to an understanding of the new concept?

Higginson summarises: 'Not only have we underestimated and failed to utilise the informal mathematics experience of young children, but we have been insufficiently sensitive to the highly arbitrary nature of many conventions and the difficulties that they present to young learners' (1983:14).

Here we have to point out that most immigrant children enter school with different pre-school experiences. The Turkish children we observed have often, owing to their cultural background and specific social situation, only limited experience of their environment, compared to the average middle-class Belgian child. Sometimes elementary experiences and activities in body movement and sensory perception are not elaborated or badly co-ordinated.

In middle-class homes a great deal of activity is spent on puzzles, games, structured material, etc. Children are involved in the most diverse events and their parents stimulate their understanding of the world. As such, much of the pre-school knowledge they obtain will prove to be useful when having to do mathematics. As we know, it is only through counting, classifying, sorting and comparing of concrete objects and different kinds of material that children will acquire insight into the concept of number. Turkish children often lack these experiences. Usually parents give their children little language practice. They consider games as mere pastimes and do not acknowledge their importance for the cognitive development of the child. This leads to the observation that Turkish immigrant children often have not acquired concepts and operations even at a rudimentary level. Therefore, in primary school attention is given to the bulk of experiences and activities that precede symbols and arithmetic.

As we pointed out above, modern mathematics too often leaves the children with abstract notions that do not relate to their environment. What these children need are activities, material and a variety of experiences. Especially for the Turkish children, one has to bear in mind that the filling and understanding of concepts starts at the level of motor activities. In this case learning mathematics starts with body and spatial explorations. They are used as a basis for verbal explicitation and the introduction of symbolic concepts.

Mathematics as a Useful Tool

Just as there is a danger in wanting to pursue the existing curriculum too much, there is also a risk in lowering the goals too drastically. Instead, a balance should be obtained between the pursuit of unattainable goals and a total lack of expectations for immigrant children. Although elementary arithmetic cannot be learned without insight, this is not the case after the first grade. Then it becomes relatively easy to let children handle numbers with a minimum of thinking and a maximum of routine and rote-learning techniques. It is often observed that, because of the vast problems immigrant children experience, a minimum level of competence is accepted. This results in a sole focus on arithmetic with a lot of stereotype exercises which demand the application of memorised algorithms instead of real insightful procedures. In this way, children are encouraged to develop a negative attitude to problem solving and prefer purely mechanical questions. As the capacity for reasoning and insight becomes more and more important in later years such situations are to be avoided. Instead, diverse cognitive functions should be practised in maths even with young children. Thus, in contrast with what is often witnessed with immigrant children, mathematics education at primary level should be more than just sums. An optimal approach should address all valuable faculties of the mind instead of limiting mathematics to rote-learned routine.

Especially for immigrant children, mathematics should be experienced as a useful instrument for making sense of the world. It can help to make children aware of their own cognitive strength. If it is used well, it leads to reflection about the world and one's own thinking and doing. Since, precisely for the immigrant child, it is necessary to cope with discrepancies between different cultural systems, mathematics can promote a style of thinking which can make it easier for the child to make sense of the different values and contexts with which it is confronted.

References

BISHOP, A.J. 1985, 'A cultural perspective on mathematics education', mimeo, Cambridge.

CUMMINS, J. 1979, 'Linguistic interdependence and the educational development of bilingual children'. *Review of Educational Research*, 49, 2, 222–51.

HIGGINSON, W. 1983, 'Threeks, rainbrellas and stunks'. In M. ZWENG, T. GREEN, *et al.* (eds), *ICME Proceedings*. Boston: Birkhauser.

HOWSON, A.G. 1983, 'Language and the teaching of mathematics'. In M. ZWENG, T. GREEN, *et al.* (eds), *ICME Proceedings*. Boston: Birkhauser.

JONES, P. 1982, 'Learning mathematics in a second language: a problem with more and less'. *Educational Studies in Mathematics*, 13, 269–87.

LLOYD, D. 1983, 'Bilingualism and mathematical reasoning in English as a second language'. *Educational Studies in Mathematics,* 14, 325–53.
OSSER, H. 1985, 'Types of knowledge in children's mathematical performances'. In F. VANDAMME and M. SPOELDERS (eds), *Discourse—Essays in Educational Pragmatics.* Leuven: C & C Acco.
SKEMP, R. 1971, *The Psychology of Learning Mathematics.* Harmondsworth: Penguin.
WILDER, R. 1981, *Mathematics as a Cultural System.* New York: Pergamon.

8 Teachers and Pupils: the Significance of Cultural Identity

MICHAEL BYRAM

It was demonstrated in an earlier chapter that parents choose to send their children to a Foyer Model school in order that the school will support their own attempts to establish an element of their own ethnic identity in their children. There are other reasons, too; for example, the potential advantage of learning Dutch. In talking about identity, however, parents emphasise the importance of children learning the language of the country of origin; in the case studied, this was Italian. The purpose of this chapter is to probe beyond the superficial characteristic of the Foyer Model as seen by parents, namely the teaching of the language of origin. For the Foyer Model is quite explicitly concerned with more than language teaching. It is a bicultural, not simply a bilingual, programme. It is, however, simultaneously a trilingual programme, introducing a complexity arising from the specific linguistic and political situation found in Brussels.

In this chapter, therefore, I shall be concerned with the specific question of the bicultural nature of the Foyer Model. I shall consider *why* the Model is explicitly bicultural in its theory and *how* it is and might be bicultural in practice. I shall examine two issues: the kind of cultural and ethnic identity envisaged in the theory of a bicultural programme and, in particular, the role of the teachers of the same origin in supporting that identity. In analysing the practices in one school, I shall consider to what extent teachers can—and might in the future—fulfil the role foreseen for them in the theory of bicultural education.

Aspects of Foyer Model Theory

The Foyer Model is unusual in its explicit theoretical discussion of the cultural dimension of programmes for immigrant children, for many such programmes often concern themselves exclusively with teaching of language. Given the intimate and inextricable relation between language and culture, it is essential that theory should not ignore the cultural dimension. In Geertz's definition (1975: 89) culture is 'an historically transmitted pattern of meanings embodied in symbols, a system of inherited conceptions expressed in a symbolic form by means of which men communicate, perpetuate and develop their knowledge about attitudes towards life'. Normally, the symbolic form which embodies culture most fully—although not to the exclusion of other symbols—is a particular language. It follows that the acquisition of a culture involves the acquisition of a language and *vice versa*. It is this kind of view which is explicit in Foyer Model theory.

The following extracts embody key concepts in the theory (all quotations are from Foyer, 1985):

> In fact the statute attributed to a 'language' in the education is more than just the choosing of a language; it is a cultural option. It is an option which has to do with the cultural identity of the future adult (p.16).

> When the language is shared with representative and vital 'carriers' of the culture of origin, then a language shared with others stabilises 'a reality' shared with one another and it has a solidarity-creating effect which leads to an acknowledged link between the members themselves (p.16).

There are three points here: (a) language is linked with and has a 'stabilising' influence on 'a reality'; (b) language is shared with others and it is the sharing which establishes the link with shared reality; (c) thus when those others are 'carriers' of another culture, the reality which is shared through language is the reality of that other culture. The assumption is that language is the necessary support for a specific cultural identity. Furthermore, it is argued that teachers 'who symbolise the culture of origin and who are as closely as possible connected to the culture of the migrant families' (p. 197) are the vital carriers of the culture who should therefore be introduced into children's lives as soon as possible.

Comparison with other situations helps to clarify and refine these statements. Consider, first, the relation of language to culture and cultural identity. On the one hand a particular language is an embodiment of a culture—through its power as a symbol system—but on the other hand it need not be used for daily communication among those who share that culture. A language may be used only on certain occasions and in specific circumstances and domains of life, rather than as the means of daily communication. In such situations, the language itself becomes a symbol (Edwards, 1977), an icon, of the culture, as well as a system of arbitrary signs embodying the culture in symbolic form. The second point of comparison is with respect to teachers. It is claimed that teachers of the same linguistic and cultural origins as immigrant children are 'carriers' of the culture, who will have a significant influence on the identity of the children. As native speakers of the language they bring the language and the culture it embodies into the lives of the children. This requires that the language be used for daily communication and not only as a symbol on special occasions. As 'carriers' of the language and culture they are significant in the lives of pupils, complementing the significance of parents.

Evidence that this view will in fact be realised in practice comes from a study of the German minority in Denmark (Byram, 1986). There are in many respects considerable differences between an 'established' (Churchill, 1986) minority and the minorities in the Foyer Model. The former has a recognised status and its own well developed system of minority schools financed by the Danish state. The latter have negligible official recognition and a bicultural programme grafted onto the majority education system. Nonetheless, it is argued in the earlier study that the ethnic identity of minority children is influenced by the fact that their teachers are of the same cultural and linguistic origin. Although children and parents talk of the significance of learning the German language, this is only the superficial view. It is the fact that the language and culture it embodies are used for daily communication and teaching within the school, which creates a school ethos influencing and shaping pupils' cultural and ethnic identity. That ethos consists of both a general sense of living in an atmosphere of German attitudes and values, and of a specific experience of being taught according to German educational and philosophical traditions (Byram, 1986:184–8). A similar view is implied in the Foyer Model.

The implicit argument of the Foyer Model is that the teaching of the language of origin by non-native speakers would not be adequate. The teachers must be natives of the culture in question. The evidence cited above supports this but also indicates how important it is that the whole school has an ethos conducive to the development of a specific cultural identity. In the Foyer Model, this is not the case. The teachers of the language of origin are only a part of the staff of the school and, unlike the German minority schools which create a minority—almost monocultural—identity, the Foyer Model is expressly bicultural. Given the dominance of the Belgian-Flemish culture, however, there is a danger that the immigrant culture will be lost or marginalised in the dominant ethos of the school. Irrespective of the 'balance' of biculturalism striven for—whether it be an equal balance or not—the fact that there are more Belgian teachers and that the curriculum is mainly Belgian, means that the culture of origin and its 'carriers' may have little or no influence.

This danger is recognised by the Foyer Model, for there is indeed evidence from similar projects that minority teachers are quickly marginalised (Boos-Nunning, 1986). Integration of minority teachers into the life of the school is crucial. At the moment, however, the integration of these teachers into the full life and structures of the school is emphasised with respect to one particular issue. This is the quest for 'intercultural education', for which 'it is important that there be present allochton and autochton teachers on the same level and in perfect co-operation'. (p.23) My argument here is that equality of status is important in the question of influencing cultural identity too. For otherwise children will quickly notice who are significant teachers and who are marginal teachers, and be influenced accordingly.

The next question to arise from this is that of the precise nature of the identity which the Model hopes to encourage in children. The issue is very complex and made even more so by the pre-existing complications of the Brussels sociolinguistic situation. The potential cultural identities, for example for Italian immigrant children, are: Sicilian, Italian, Italian-Belgian, Italo-Flemish Belgian, Italo-French Belgian and perhaps other combinations. In the Italian case, the difference between Standard Italian and Sicilian dialect is a further complicating factor which the immigrants bring with them into the Brussels situation. The key statement by Foyer on cultural identity is:

As a thesis we would like to put forward that supporting a (after all real) subjective cultural identity does not necessarily have to be a disadvantage, neither for the social adjustment of the persons involved nor for their loyalty towards the host land and its inhabitants' (p.18)

This when added to earlier statements on the role of the language of origin in creating cultural identity would seem to suggest that some kind of hyphenated identity is envisaged. It is, of course, possible for the identity to change over time, with shifting emphasis and through change in the form of experience, including linguistic experience.

There is thus still room for further refinement in Foyer Model theory with respect to the kind of identity it is hoped to encourage. The case of Italian children of Sicilian origin and the disparity between Standard Italian and Sicilian dialect is not atypical of migrant workers who often originate from peripheral regions of their country with strong regional identities and salient linguistic characteristics. At this point, however, we turn to the realisation of

Foyer Model theory in practice, and in particular in one school taken as a case-study, i.e. one of the schools with an Italian programme.

Teachers as 'Carriers' of Culture

There are a number of ways in which minority teachers realise their role in shaping children's identity:

—most obviously, they teach the language of origin,

—they introduce the educational traditions and philosophies of the country of origin into the Belgian school,

—they create links between school and minority parents and complement the influence of parents on identity,

—they introduce a minority culture content to the curriculum.

One teacher described the teaching of Italian as follows:

'le but, ce n'est pas tellement d'enseigner la langue italienne, mais c'est à travers la langue italienne et la connaissance de l'Italie de donner une identité aux enfants'.

The teaching of the language of origin, it has been argued above, inevitably involves the teaching of culture. Similarly, the precise nature of the language learning involved for any particular pupil or group of pupils also indicates what kind of cultural learning is taking place. Although Foyer Model theory uses the term 'mother tongue', where children are second or third generation, born in Belgium, this concept is in particular need of explication. As was evident from a previous chapter, the amount and nature of Italian spoken by pupils outside school Italian lessons is varied and complex. For many pupils, French is the dominant language in terms of frequency of use and range of experience, even if Italian has a special affective role in pupils' lives. Teachers cannot therefore assume they can teach Italian language and culture as if they were teaching children in Italy. Even if Italian were dominant, the language and culture of an Italian minority in Belgium gradually develop their own characteristics and differ from the language and culture of Italy. On the other hand, teachers cannot use the methods of teaching a foreign language and culture, since these would be plainly inappropriate for children who frequently go to Italy, speak some Italian at home, and already have some sense of being Italian. Methods and techniques have to be developed for the specific situation and consequently there are considerable professional demands on teachers to adapt and innovate.

One aspect of this kind of language teaching is often overlooked. Monolingual children begin to develop an affective as well as cognitive use of their language from an early age. They sing songs, hear poems and rhymes, express their emotions and needs, in their language. This is a fundamentally significant dimension of their acquisition of a culture through language; they acquire the shared cultural values and meanings. If the language of origin is to play a similar part in the shaping of minority children's cultural identity, this affective, expressive experience has to be present, too. If, however, their cognitive control of the language is noticeably weak—as is the case for many second-generation children—then there is a tendency to seek to remedy this 'problem' and to underplay the techniques and opportunities which will develop the affective dimension. It may even be a tacit assumption that children cannot be expected to respond to such teaching until they have a more developed cognitive control of the (standard) language. Yet the importance of helping pupils to develop an attachment to the language of origin—a sense of the poetic function of their language—cannot be exaggerated.

A second way in which minority teachers influence school and pupils is through their presence as representatives of an educational tradition. This is much less evident in the daily routine of school than is the language teaching. It is not as significant in the overt curriculum as in the 'hidden curriculum' of values and attitudes to learning and childhood—what was above called the ethos of the school. It is not always without problems, since it may be in contrast or even conflict with the Belgium educational ethos. The following description is based on interviews with Italian teachers. It is a paraphrase and summary of their views, including some direct quotations.

There are differences in the two approaches to teaching. This is not to say that one is better and one worse, but simply that there are differences: 'une autre façon de voir les choses'. Given the freedom due to absence of a specified curriculum for Italian, the approach is to adapt the lesson to the responses of the pupils on a particular occasion, to allow the pupils greater freedom to move about in the classroom, to put more emphasis on speaking rather than writing and use of worksheets. From this perspective, Belgian traditions seem rigid and strict, deciding on what shall be taught in advance rather than allowing the pupils to influence the content of the lesson. The Belgian tradition is more systematic and there are advantages and disadvantages in both approaches.

There are also differences between approaches in Italy and Belgium. A symptom of these differences is the way in which pupil reports are done in primary schools in Italy and Belgium. In Italy parents are given written descriptions or reports about their children's work, perhaps a paragraph of writing, and are not given marks or percentages for each subject. From this perspective, the Belgian system again seems rigid and too exact, although this is not to say that pupils are not given marks for their work in the Italian tradition; simply that the way of reporting to parents is different.

In such a situation the teachers feel that they have to adapt to Belgian procedures. With respect to expectations of discipline, for example, a small but significant requirement that pupils must line up in the school yard before going into class was felt to be contrary to the Italian approach. It was nonetheless recognised that Italian teachers had to insist on this, too, in order to be consistent. This is one of the small but symptomatic signs of the hidden curriculum of values and relationships which differs between Italian and Belgian approaches. It suggests that Italian teachers suppress some of their own traditions and, as a consequence, their influence on the ethos and on pupils' identity is lessened, although not necessarily completely removed. The very fact that they are present as full-time members of staff, integrated into the normal curriculum of the school, is significant for pupils and parents.

The relationship of minority teachers with parents is very important. It is one of the aims of the Foyer Model to help parents to become more integrated into Belgian society through co-operation with schools. Again, teachers' interviews are helpful:

The difficulties created by cultural difference are made more complex by the level of education of many of the Italian parents, which means through no fault of theirs that they do not have a proper understanding of the worries and problems of Belgian teachers with their children. Yet this cannot be solved by Foyer acting as mediator. There has to be direct communication between parents and teachers in the school. On the other hand the linguistic barriers are very high, even if French is used, and there is often a need for the Italian teacher in the school to act as interpreter— not just to interpret linguistically but also culturally. Furthermore, it is possible that Belgian teachers do not realise sufficiently just how little Italian parents can help their children with schoolwork, again not simply because of their not understanding Dutch but because of their own lack of education.

The dependence of all parents without a high level of education on the school as a source of help for their children is particularly marked in some minority parents. The major disruptive experience of migration—even if it took place in an older generation—is not undertaken lightly. To leave one's home requires a drive and ambition to improve one's destiny. For those who have succeeded in the initial stage of finding work and an adequate economic foothold, the next stage is to improve one's situation within the new environment. This was evident in some Italian parents, particularly those who are second generation: they hope for social advancement for their children. As for others at the lower end of the social system, education is seen as an escape from present circumstances for the next generation:

Mother: Ah oui, nos parents ne parlaient pas du tout français. Ils ont travaillé dans les mines, nos parents . . .
Father: Nous on a eu l'handicap que . . . eux ils ne parlaient pas le français . . . ils ne pouvaient pas nous aider . . . ils n'ont pas su nous aider . . . enfin, on n'a pas eu la même chance que nos enfants, quoi.
Mother: Enfin . . . pour eux c'est le néerlandais, maintenant Enfin, quand on peut l'aider, on l'aide quoi. Tandis que nous . . . avec nos parents . . . c'était impossible, quoi.

It is evident that there are two overlapping functions. Italian teachers have the role of supporting Italian identity. They are also seen as mediators between parents' and parental ambitions and the school as an instrument for realising those ambitions.

The fourth way in which minority teachers influence the school ethos is, like language teaching, visible in the overt curriculum. The introduction of 'inter-cultural education' into the curriculum is an explicit part of Foyer Model theory, as is the role of minority teachers in this part of the curriculum, as cited above. In the case-study school this theory had been interpreted in terms of making both Italian and Belgian pupils familiar with aspects of Italian and Belgian life. There is a danger that this leads to tokenism and folklore—a danger recognised by Italian teachers:

There is no appropriate material available and the definition of what intercultural education is and what its purposes are remains unclear. Culture is not so much knowledge of geography and history but rather a 'mentalité', and there are dangers in emphasising aspects of Italian life which are to be found only as 'mauvais folklore' and not representative of modern Italy. The best intercultural education comes from working together, from comparing and contrasting both Flemish and Italian culture, from emphasizing what is common rather than different. There is no reason for forcing knowledge of Italy onto Belgian pupils, but rather there should be a sharing of knowledge about each other's culture, whether it is in questions of food, or architecture or whatever else.

Belgian teachers feel even more ill at ease with the concept.

In principle, however, this is a very important part of the minority teacher's work. For, if they are to have some impact on school ethos, this is the one area of the curriculum where that impact can extend beyond the specific issue of language teaching and beyond their relationship with Italian children. They can affect the curriculum for all children and also be involved in a teaching relationship with Belgian pupils. If, moreover, the intercultural education lessons are taught by both Italian and Belgian teachers, the formal integration of minority teachers into the staffing structure will be complemented by an actual co-operation in working methods and approaches which may have influence on the hidden curriculum and the school ethos.

Affective Use of Language in the Current Model

The Foyer Model in its current state of development falls into two parts. In the kindergarten and the first two years of primary school, Italian pupils follow a different timetable from that of Belgian pupils. A large proportion of their curriculum is 'Italian'. This means that some of their lessons are concerned with the language as the object of instruction and in others Italian serves as the medium of instruction. In the first primary year, more than half the lessons are Italian; in the second year, just under a third are Italian. The move to the third year, however, marks an important change: essentially Italian and Belgian pupils have the same timetable but Italian children are withdrawn for three or four lessons of Italian. The change is significant not only in the drop in the number of lessons but also in that the language from that moment becomes only an object rather than a medium of learning.

The significance of the distinction between language as object and language as medium has not yet been fully recognised. As a consequence, the opportunities for developing children's affective attachment to Italian are not fully realised. It is present in pupils' relations with Italian teachers, with whom they speak Italian during and outside lessons, and the importance of the presence of Italian teachers is again evident in this. On the other hand, the use of Italian as medium in lessons such as music, art and crafts would also strengthen children's affective associations of the language with diverse experience of the environment in which they live. Something of this takes place in the early years but is lost after the second year when Italian is largely an object of learning.

The withdrawal system is recognised by all those involved as problematic, although at the moment the only practical solution. The system tends to marginalise both the subject and the teacher. It takes pupils away from precisely those lessons—music, art, craft—in which their affective development is pursued in the medium of Dutch. On the other hand the belief that they need to learn to read and write the standard Italian language means that in the few lessons of Italian, there is little time for affective use of the language. Time has to be spent on developing pupils' cognitive control of the written language.

It may be possible in the future to introduce modifications in the Foyer Model which would create greater integration of the minority language and culture in the later years of primary schooling. One possibility would be to continue to use the minority language as medium by teaching some music or art in parallel with music and art lessons in Dutch for the Belgian pupils. The extension of the notion of team-teaching in 'intercultural education' to include using both Dutch and Italian as media of teaching and learning would underline the importance of Italian and Italian teachers as integral to the main curriculum of the school. Such possibilities remain to be explored.

It is notoriously difficult, if not impossible, to measure or estimate the contribution of education to pupils' academic success. It is all the more difficult to analyse how education influences identity. Objective, measurable evidence is unlikely to be available. It is rather a question of trust in a rational and well developed theory, used as a basis for influencing practice. The theory that native-speaker teachers are essential as carriers of culture is reasonable, given what we know about language and culture and the process of language acquisition. The practices of the Foyer Model are such that pupils are placed in situations in the early years where they form significant relationships with these carriers of culture. It is reasonable to suppose that the relationships will form a propitious environment in which their minority identity will be reinforced. On the other hand, the integration of minority teachers and minority teaching into the life and structures of the school is not complete, and the importance of the poetic function of language, and of the use of language as a medium of learning, is yet to be fully realised in theory and in practice. It is in these dimensions of language teaching that the native speaker and carrier of culture is especially valuable. It is here that the cultural identity of the teacher may have most influence on the cultural identity of the pupil.

References

BOOS-NUNNING, J. et al. 1986, Towards intercultural education: a comparative study of the education of migrant children in Belgium, England, France and the Netherlands. London: CILT.
BYRAM, M.S. 1986, Minority Education and Ethnic Survival. Clevedon: Multilingual Matters.
CHURCHILL, S. 1986, The Education of Linguistic and Cultural Minorities in the OECD Countries. Clevedon: Multilingual Matters.
EDWARDS, J. 1977, Ethnic identity and bilingual education. In HOWARD GILES (ed.), Language, Ethnicity and Intergroup Relations, 253–82. London: Academic Press.
FOYER, 1985, Four Years' Bicultural Education in Brussels. Brussels: Foyer.
GEERTZ, C. 1975, The Interpretation of Cultures. London: Hutchinson.

9 Structural Change: from Monocultural to Bicultural Schools

LUDO SMEEKENS

The description of structural effects of an extensive and complex programme, as is the case for the bicultural projects of Foyer in Brussels, is not an easy task, if one bears in mind that it is an extended project which cannot be implemented as such in a school. On the contrary, the organisation and introduction of a bicultural education programme is rather a process, in which one and the same theme of innovation should grow, involving all interested parties.

The aim of this contribution is to give a description of the bicultural projects from the point of view of this process of innovation and the related problems. Following Van den Berg and Vandenberghe (1984), we shall review the features and problems of this innovation project, considering five aspects. First we shall look at the innovation project, with reference to the stated educational aims and we shall see to what extent all this may be considered as innovation. Secondly, the school will be looked upon as being an organisation. It is important to consider the features of the school as an organisation, and to see how these characteristics may influence the implementation of the bicultural projects. On a third level we shall discuss the importance of the teacher in a bicultural project, with some extra attention paid to the features of teachers as individuals and their involvement in the innovation.

A fourth subject of discussion will be the structure of supervision of the bicultural project. Major questions are how the supervision is conceived and to what extent it facilitates the implementation.

136

Finally, in a fifth point, we shall try to explain in what way the local and national policies facilitate or hinder the management of bicultural projects.

The Aims of the Innovation Project

In the planning of the bicultural project, a multitude of objects was determined, which now may be described by means of three major ideas (for detailed description of the project's aims and model of education, see the contribution by Leman, at the beginning of this publication):

a. The creation of an intercultural perspective within the school and the promotion of the intercultural way of acting by the teacher.

b. The improvement of learning results, i.e. reducing the arrears (in terms of the learning process) of immigrant children, through the development of new educational techniques and strategies.

c. The involvement of the immigrant community(ies) in the Flemish cultural life and Flemish community structures via a societal subsystem, which is education.

a. Creating an intercultural perspective and promoting an intercultural way of teaching

This objective is related to the school as meso-structure, in the sense that the Flemish school, that in essence addresses the average Flemish middle-class pupil, should be adapted to the social reality in Brussels. Considering the fact that only one newborn baby out of ten comes from a Flemish family, that five out of ten are born in immigrant families and four out of ten babies are of French-speaking Belgian origin, a one-sided directedness to the Flemish pupil can only evoke serious problems (Leman, 1988).

The conception of the bicultural projects was strongly influenced by the vision of Foyer based on both the societal phenomenon which Brussels represents and on the phenomenon of integration. Without any doubt the support of the proper cultural identity is a necessary condition to be able to reach a successful and real integration.

From our point of view, Brussels may be considered as a multicultural and multilingual city, in which the Flemish community holds a minority position (quantitatively speaking). Consequently, the support of the cultural identity of both immigrants and Flemish people has become a necessity and an important condition for a balanced and harmonious society in Brussels (Smeekens & de Smedt, 1987).

In relation to this aim of the innovation, i.e. creating an intercultural perspective, two dimensions are clearly distinguished. First there is a broadening of perspective, from the monocultural into the intercultural and secondly a deepening and accentuation of the Flemish identity. Both components are very important, in terms of innovation in the Flemish school.

b. *Developing new teaching techniques and strategies*

This aim concerns both the individual way of teaching of the teacher and his or her functioning as a member of the school team. Within a bicultural project, in which the proper language of immigrants takes a fairly central place and amount of time, one cannot avoid a reformulation and re-ordering of educational goals. This process concerns the whole team: goals that cannot be realised at a particular level have to be postponed until a later level. Certain educational goals will already be reached via the teaching in the immigrant language. Some goals will lose importance while others will gain, owing to the new educational perspective. The process of defining goals and giving them a concrete form requires a great amount of reflection on the part of the teacher and needs a lot of forethought in the team.

Secondly, from the moment goals are defined and given a concrete formulation, adequate techniques and strategies need to be developed, in order to be able to realise the objectives. A striking example of this process of reorientation, the reformulation of instructional goals, with a major change of teaching strategies included, is the subject 'Nederlands' (Dutch). Until the moment of introduction of immigrant pupils into the schools where the project was organised, Dutch had generally been considered as the mother tongue, regardless of whether this coincided with the linguistic reality of the children or not (quite a lot of pupils have a French speaking background, even if they go to Flemish schools). The linguistic concept 'mother tongue' had always been part and parcel of the Flemish school itself, which considered Dutch as *its* mother tongue. The linguistic reality of the children plays hardly a part in this view (Jaspaert & Lemmens, 1987). One of the sub-aims of bicultural education is precisely to reformulate the goals for Dutch language teaching in the elementary school.

The essence of this second aim of innovation lies in the fact that teachers themselves must learn to be responsible for both what and how to teach. They should also realise that teaching in an innovation project is a creative act for which neither experience nor ready made pedagogical programmes can give all the answers.

c. The involvement of the immigrant community in Flemish societal life

This third aim of the process of innovation is probably less a strict instructional matter and the most generally formulated object of this project. It rather concerns relationships between different communities in Brussels and the function of education within this context.

In Brussels there actually is a vast distance between the Flemish and the immigrant communities. Foyer considers this as a negative evolution for both communities. This distance may on the one hand be partly explained by linguistic factors and partly by the fact that the Flemish community in Brussels is smaller and more self-centred. On the other hand, the immigrant communities orientate usually towards the French-speaking community in Brussels. This can be explained by the dominance of the French language in the street and because of the prestige that French maintains in the country of origin. The immigrants use French community structures, accept French as language of socialisation most of the time and send their children to French schools. Nevertheless, in Brussels the Flemish community is gaining in interest with Flemish economic and numerical dominance on the national level. An obvious consequence is the growing importance of Dutch, rather as a source of identity than as a means of communication. Having a knowledge of Dutch, one can prove to belong to a new, prestigious élite, the bilinguals (Dutch-French).

Within this specific framework, a possibility of self-improvement by obtaining more attractive jobs is created. This is the main reason why immigrant communities gain interest in being involved in the Flemish community and, doing so, avoid extra difficulties. However, the Flemish community also has an interest in this integration of a number of immigrant children. Within a European context, multilingualism may be considered as a 'must'. A lack of collaboration and involvement from both immigrants and Flemings would mean a missed opportunity in terms of multilingualism.

There is still more. Should the immigrant community living in Brussels ever get into a worse social and economic position, the Flemish community would—rightly or wrongly—be accused of leading an élitist policy, by not allowing the immigrant population to participate in Flemish societal life.

The perspective of innovation for the school lies in the fact that it is in the best position to stimulate this reciprocal involvement, precisely because education is considered as an institutional way of transferring values and culture. The innovation aspect is that the perspective is enlarged: whereas cultural transfer in a school used to be an exclusive one-way process, now it has to be considered as a mutual process.

Summarising bicultural education as a project of innovation, three general objectives were mentioned. It is important that every objective can be given a concrete form in many sub-goals: little projects of innovation in larger wholes of innovation, so to speak, which should be carried out at the same time.

Related to this, Van den Berg and Vandenberghe (1984) introduce the idea of a multi-dimensionality of pedagogical innovations. They claim that a multitude of interpretations on the contents of innovation is left to the people involved, both referring to the choice of priorities and the filling-in of particular dimensions, as regards contents. Moreover, Foyer considers also that the supervising team can share varying interpretations of priorities and accents and thus influence the different teams of teachers. It will be clear that the realisation of the bicultural innovation project will differ in every school, keeping in mind the features of the process of implementation and the multi-dimensionality of the content of innovation.

Features of the Organisation of the School

In the bicultural projects of Foyer, the school itself as a social structure is the subject of changes. In order to achieve this, a great number of aims are pursued simultaneously. These objectives are certainly not always very clear or presented in a concrete form. Moreover, they are not always adjusted to everyday class reality. Nonetheless, their realisation requires the involvement of many people, both in and out of the school (school authorities, head of the school, supervising team, inspection). Corbett gives these changes a name: 'high scope changes', as opposed to 'low scope changes' (Corbett, 1981). He describes the criteria mainly in terms of the extent to which a planned change is linked with class reality and in terms of the number of people involved. In his analysis he refers to the type of organisation of a school, when he claims that the more the school shows features of a loosely coupled organisation, the more difficult the realisation of high scope changes becomes.

At the implementation of its bicultural projects, Foyer expected to come across schools organised in such a way as to be able to handle a complex process of innovation. Foyer assumed that the schools would form a relatively coherent whole, in which decisions were made on the basis of analysis of facts and the creative search for alternatives, a process of making conclusions in which the school team maintains a central position. The role of the school-head was considered to be of a pedagogical and supervisory nature, a kind of inside stand-by. Further, Foyer was convinced that teachers would undoubtedly be able to keep in mind the school functioning as an organisation, and not only the learning results of the children. Foyer expected, in other words, teachers to be organisation-minded.

A number of factors explain these assumptions of Foyer. In the first place, Foyer did not have much experience with implementing rather extended projects of innovation, at least not beyond its own organisation. The lack of experience could not entirely be compensated by the know-how of other institutes. Although Belgium is endowed with an extended net of the so-called P.M.S.-services (psycho-medical-social services), these almost only point out individual learning problems. Other organisations, which might function only in terms of school guidance, simply do not exist. The sociocultural sector, of which Foyer is part, had never had any special intervention in the field of education: organisations which were not closely linked with schools had already realised that the education system is rather a closed system. Many social workers complain that they cannot easily get access to a school, even before any intervention was suggested.

Finally, Foyer itself is a rather coherent and solid structure. Relations within the staff are clearly defined, so that decision-making can be dealt with quickly and efficiently. From its position as a private organisation Foyer continuously has to adjust to new circumstances in the immigrant sector and is obliged to come up with new, creative alternatives.

All these factors made Foyer think in a particular way about the schools which wanted to participate in the project. During the first period in which the Foyer projects were started, Foyer was not able to put its expectations to the test of reality. At the outset, the department of education was not inclined to acknowledge the project as an experiment, which resulted in the fact that the project remained marginal and that Foyer members were unable to establish a well-structured bond with the school. At this time the project could hardly have been defined as an innovation project creating structural changes. Moreover, each project started on a very small scale. In the first and second grade, immigrant pupils were separated from the other children, for the greater part. Only from the third grade on was the project anchored in the school structure. During the third year, schools started to change. The first signs of tension among teachers and between the school and Foyer became obvious. Questions such as 'Is this still our school?' were often raised.

Our conception of school organisation has been strongly influenced by the theory on curriculum development in the Netherlands (Van Vilsteren, 1984) and by the understanding of the school as a loosely-coupled organisation (Weick, 1982). In the first place, we discovered that schools usually do not consider the functions of their own organisation and the realisation of well-defined organisational objectives (as opposed to the objectives of education to be realised by the pupils). Generally, teachers feel less involved with the school as an organisation than with the weals and woes of their pupils. From our experience we learned that few schools are able to formulate their objective as an organisation and that teachers do not or hardly ever feel motivated to reflect about such objectives. Generally, teachers have confidence in the professional qualities of their colleagues, which is observed in a lack of exchange of information. When eventually decision-making related to the school as a whole is established, these decisions are not always actually carried out. Organisations of this type of structure can be considered as being loosely coupled. Events which occur in one part of the system do not necessarily influence other parts of the system, nor the whole. If suddenly the school has to work in completely new circumstances which are different from everyday practice, these circumstances bring about far-reaching consequences. New work circumstances mentioned earlier as 'high scope changes' and of which the bicultural project is certainly an example, need an organisation with a tightly coupled structure. The more organisations have a loosely coupled structure, the less high scope changes can be implemented (Weick, 1982).

In Brussels, three factors influence the structural features of schools. Firstly, the involvement of teachers with the objectives of the school is not without problems, since most of the teachers live in (monolingual Flemish) municipalities around Brussels. This results in the fact that they live in a reality which is totally different from the school reality and its natural population. Secondly, the Belgian teacher is less inclined (in comparison with his Dutch colleagues, for example) to consider himself as a member of a group, at least not in the sense of a functional collaboration. Lastly, in the tradition of Belgian schools, the school principal does not consider it as a very important matter to create or stimulate such a functional team as mentioned above. He considers himself rather as an administrator who looks after the everyday course of things.

In respect of a project of innovation like the bicultural project, we can state that the type of organisation of the Brussels school hinders rather than facilitates the implementation process. The supervising team, Foyer in this case, should therefore also work on teambuilding and structural features of the school, rather than being involved only with the innovation itself. A central point is the way organisational objectives should be (re-)defined, in concert with the school management and teachers.

The Individual Teachers

Foyer has the conviction that the individual teacher is the axis round which educational innovation turns. This does not mean that the success of an innovation programme depends only on the teacher. We consider the interaction between the school and the supervising team as well as the teacher are important factors of success.

Different teachers are involved in different ways in the bicultural projects. Foreign teachers are responsible for teaching in the mother tongue while others are responsible for teaching Dutch as a second language. Teachers of the higher grades of elementary school are more directed to the concrete learning result in function of the secondary school than teachers of the lower grades. All teachers judge and interpret the innovation project from that background: personal experiences in the past, their concrete work perspective and the place they occupy in the school structure. It is obvious that the supervising team should be conscious of the variation of interpretation of the project that the different teachers have. Byram's description of the different interpretations in one of the project schools in his evaluation study is illuminative for this (Byram, 1987). The supervising team should not conceive these different interpretations and senses as the expression of irrationality on the part of the teachers, as opposed to the rationality of the supervisors. The whole of these interpretations and senses should on the contrary be conceived as defining the possibilities of innovation, and as a starting-point for interventions by the supervising team. In this sense Fullan can easily be understood when he is pleading for the taking into account of the subjective elements of educational innovation and when he claims that 'the trans-formation of subjective realities is the essence of change' (Fullan, 1982: 28).

In the process of transformation of subjective realities the foreign teachers share a special position. Their position in the staff, their permanent possibilities of interaction with the other teachers and their growing insight in the concrete interpretation of the project by the other teachers have given them a pivot function in the transformation process. The foreign teacher should fully realise the importance of his role in this process. The meaning of this with respect to the implementation of bicultural education will be clear. One of the major objectives of the supervision will therefore be the expansion of the interpersonal skills of the foreign teachers. Foyer organises regular meetings with the foreign teachers of different schools at which these matters are discussed. The information and the transfer of 'know-how' is very useful, not only for the foreign teachers themselves but also for the members of the supervising team.

The Supervision

In previous paragraphs we have already made clear that the implementation of the bicultural project was meant as a process for the supervising team too. A process in which the ideas about the content of the project, about the organisational features of the school and about the teacher as an individual are to be adjusted constantly.

The original strategy of Foyer was to realise the implementation of bicultural education in the shape of a 'dissemination' process. Foyer started out from the point of view that if a number of formal interventions were carried out at the organisational level and at the level of teaching techniques, the desired transformations of subjective realities would occur spontaneously. The most important formal interventions were: the introduction of a fairly large number of immigrant children, two or three foreign teachers and a changed curriculum (for the immigrant children, anyway). The Foyer model was presented as a rounded whole which can be implemented as such in a school, and on which the school could base its adjustment of objectives, types of co-operation between teachers, and changes in the rest of the curriculum; a kind of dissemination process. The most important job of the supervising team would therefore be to hold this bicultural nucleus and occasionally check the effects on the rest of the organisation. This one-sided concentration on the bicultural nucleus in the school was partly the result of practical circumstances. Almost the whole curriculum for the immigrant children had to be constructed from the beginning. Teaching techniques for a model of this kind were not available and the foreign teachers did not have any experience in this way of functioning as a teacher.

After some time, when the practical difficulties were finished with, the supervision got more and more orientated to the school as such and could adjust to this or that particular school. Supervision became less a matter of adapting the school to the aims of innovation, but more a matter of adapting the project to the innovation perspective of the school.

Summing up, we can state that related to this the school supervising team is faced with the supervising of a process rather than with the carrying out of a number of measures or with introducing teaching techniques. Moreover, our experience was that the guidance got more effective the more the supervising team worked in the real class practice and the more they arranged contact between teachers working on the same aspects of innovation. Foyer considers the supervising team's task to be creating circumstances in which teachers, sharing one innovation theme, can meet.

The Policy of Innovation

Bicultural education as a project of innovation was conceived by a private organisation, Foyer, and not by the regular school authorities. One of the objectives of Foyer at the conception of these projects was the stimulation of the authorities to work on a coherent policy of immigrant education. The objective was to create a number of pilot-schools from which alternative solutions could be presented. It is important to keep this perspective in mind. It means that Foyer pursues a proper objective in the realisation of the bicultural projects, which exceeds the concrete school. The process of innovation hereby gets a specific colour.

From this viewpoint, the bicultural project contains two dimensions: one is the process of innovation within the schools and the second is the process of innovation within a broader context of educational policy which is defined by the authorities. From our point of view, this second dimension should also be explicit to all those involved. So far this has hardly been the case, because Foyer considered this dimension as an organisational objective from Foyer itself. Nevertheless, it showed that this aim influences the process of implementation of the bicultural projects. As a matter of fact, it gives it a broader perspective.

In summary, we can state that in the light of the realisation of an innovation project, the organisation which conceptualises and implements such a project should analyse and explain its own aims accurately.

In this contribution we have described the bicultural project as an innovation project. We tried to show that bicultural education is a complex matter, in which different goals should be realised simultaneously. The multidimensionality of the project's aims was a central element in the description. Above all, it was our intention to show that the implementation of a project such as bicultural education is to be considered as a continuous process, in which one's own ideas and interpretations should be adjusted constantly. Moreover, we wanted to show that a bicultural project is not a uniform, finished product, but on the contrary differs from school to school.

References

BYRAM, M. 1987, *The Foyer Bicultural Education Model: an Evaluation*. Durham: University of Durham.
CORBETT, H.D. 1981, *Organizational coupling and the implementation of planned school change*. Paper presented at the annual conference of the American Educational Research Association, Los Angeles.

FULLAN, M. 1982, *The Meaning of Educational Change*. New York: Teachers College Press.

JASPAERT, K. and LEMMENS, G. 1987, *Evaluatie van het Nederlands in het Foyer bicultureel onderwijsproject*. Tilburg: Katholieke Universiteit Brabant.

LEMAN, J. 1988, 'Het bicultureel onderwijs in Vlaamse basisscholen te Brussel'. *Ons Erfdeel* 31, 1, 83–86.

SMEEKENS, L. and DE SMEDT, H. 1987, 'Het Nederlands in Brussel: Tweede taal of Vreemde taal?' In G. EXTRA, R. VAN HOUT and T. VALLEN, *Etnische minderheden: Taalverwerving, Taalonderwijs, Taalbeleid*. Dordrecht: Foris.

VAN DEN BERG, R. and VANDENBERGHE, R. 1984, *Grootschaligheid in de onderwijsvernieuwing*. Tilburg: Zwijsen.

VAN VILSTEREN, C.A. 1984, 'De school als professioneel-bureaucratische organisatie'. *Handboek Schoolorganisatie en Onderwijsmanagement*. Alphen a/d Rijn: Samson.

WEICK, K.E. 1982, 'Administering education in loosely coupled schools'. *Phi Delta Kappan*, 673–76.

10 Looking to the Future

MICHAEL BYRAM and JOHAN LEMAN

Introduction

As we said in our introduction, the purpose of this book is to present the Foyer Model in its present state of development. The Model arose out of a specific combination of circumstances and has been constantly modified and refined as circumstances changed. The original foundation was laid by organisations of Italian and Spanish parents (the 'Cittadinanza Migrante' and the 'Centro Socio-Cultural Español') and subsequently, for Turkish and Moroccan projects, under the auspices of 'Dar al Amal', one of the larger organisations for immigrant women in Brussels. The dynamic of the Model's development has since then been influenced by teachers and other educationalists, including those contributing to this volume. There are indications that political events will also very soon bring another source of change to bear. It has been one of the merits of the Foyer Model that it has recognised and anticipated the evolution of education for immigrants. The task for the future will be to embrace further modifications and anticipate the next phases of change in the circumstances in which the Model functions. The capacity to combine theoretical change with a pragmatic and accurate analysis of those circumstances will be crucial in the longer term future of the Model and the various projects.

This final chapter is thus an attempt to look into the future: to discuss change in the Model and change in the socio-political environment of Brussels in which the Model must function. We shall consider first the issues which confront us in the short term, and then turn to the wider questions of the future of immigrants in Brussels and the consequences for the education system.

Refining and Developing the Foyer Model

Three questions have been raised for the immediate future: the development of an adequate methodology for the teaching of French, the desirability

147

of teaching the first stages of mathematics in the 'mother tongue' and the relationship between the 'mother tongue' and school subjects which depend upon and contribute to children's affective, emotional development.

Methods of teaching French in Dutch-speaking schools have traditionally treated French as a foreign language, with which pupils have little or no familiarity. Outside Brussels this has been and still is a reasonable approach. Teachers in Brussels primary schools, however, find themselves in a different situation: all children live in an environment where French is dominant in the public sphere, and many children—especially immigrant second or third generation—use French frequently in both public and private. A foreign language teaching methodology is not appropriate and teachers do indeed make pragmatic changes to their techniques of teaching. There is nonetheless a continuing need for refinement, for appropriate teaching materials, for techniques and methods which take into account the real situation, using children's existing knowledge and drawing on the linguistic environment in which they live.

The teaching of the 'mother tongue' or language of origin has been deliberately associated in the Model with the teaching of subjects with high cognitive demands and with high status in the eyes of teachers and parents alike. Mathematics has a higher prestige than music; reading and writing are seen as more significant than painting or drawing. As a consequence it can be argued that children's linguistic development in the language of origin is unbalanced, with insufficient attention paid to associating the language with experience in subjects which encourage and guide their affective development. There is an evident need for further investigation, both empirical and theoretical, of this issue in the near future.

The teaching of mathematics in the 'mother tongue' has been a fundamental characteristic of the Model since its inception. Yet the theoretical arguments—discussed in Chapter 7 by Snoeck—have also to be related to pragmatic developments. Discussion of the teaching of mathematics has been prominent in the contributions by practising teachers in several projects, and the extension of the Model to a project for Moroccan children has brought the question even more into focus. Hitherto, our attention has been largely turned to children of broadly European origin—Italian, Spanish, Turkish—but our concern for Moroccan children raises new issues, of which mathematics teaching is one.

The sociolinguistic environment of the Moroccans is clearly more complex: they tend to be more insular in their settlement patterns in Brussels; their relationship to French, as an important language in the country of origin, is different; the significance of classical Arabic and Moroccan Arabic is complicated by religious questions. In this situation the need to adapt the Model in the light of both theory and pragmatism, characteristic of earlier phases, is even more evident. As a consequence in kindergarten only one third of the time is spent in Arabic and Dutch is used for the rest.

In the first two years of primary education, eight hours per week will be given in Arabic: two hours to Arabic as a language and six hours to religion, culture, singing, expression and current affairs. In the third and fourth years, seven hours per week will be divided into two hours for the Arabic language and five hours for religion, culture, singing and current affairs in Arabic. In the last two years, we have opted for four hours in Arabic, of which two hours will be devoted to the Arabic language and two hours in Arabic for religion and culture.

This means that mathematics, as such, will not be given in Arabic, although it is explicitly planned that the most important concepts will be taught simultaneously in the Arabic language classes. This also means that, in comparison with the other projects, more Dutch is planned for the first years and proportionally somewhat more Arabic from the third year on. The more complex linguistic situation of these children requires these changes. As in the other projects, French is taught from the third year on.

In essence the changes discussed so far are part of the continuous monitoring of the Model as it develops in specific projects. Other modifications may soon be required as the patterns of immigration and settlement change. It is quite likely, although not yet certain, that movement of immigrants will spread throughout the Brussels agglomeration and the ghetto-like concentrations of the present will be different. Ethnic groups will mix in specific areas of Brussels and it will as a consequence be less possible or desirable to organise projects for just one ethnic group per school. This will constitute a major new challenge: how can the important characteristics of the present structure be maintained whilst the Model is modified in a number of features in order to cope with a school population comprising more than one ethnic group in addition to Flemish Belgians? One important factor will be the size and distribution of Dutch-language schools in Brussels and the number of Flemish people for which they cater. Another will be the actual composition of the catchment areas in which they are situated.

Another kind of challenge lies in the development of the Model into the secondary school. The first group of Italian children has recently left primary school and their experience in secondary will be carefully monitored. As more and more children graduate from primary into secondary the individual attention will have to be systematised and new structures created. This poses challenges for Foyer management and for teachers alike.

Changes in Educational Context

Slowly but surely the changing character of Brussels as a city is gaining public recognition. The figures cited in Chapter 1 are beginning to have an impact on politicians and public opinion. Brussels is becoming, from a statutory point of view, a multicultural and even multilingual city, and the value of other European languages in a city which is not just the capital of Belgium but of Europe is being recognised. The longer term consequences will be significant not least for the education system in general and for the education of immigrants in particular.

What will this mean for minorities of whatever origin? What effect will this development have upon the creation and maintenance of minority identities, on the potential for hyphenated identities such as Italian-Belgian or Moroccan-Belgian? What will be the future of Dutch in this complex sociolinguistic situation? Such questions are not easy to answer in general other than by speculation, but there are some more specific indications of educational needs and the potential contribution of the Foyer Model.

There is no doubt that the internationalisation of Brussels has immediate implications for Dutch-speaking schools, with or without a Foyer project in their midst. All teachers in such schools need to be made aware of the particular problems and techniques of teaching Dutch to immigrant children. This is a unique situation which calls for new and unique methods, such as those developed in the Foyer Model. In a similar vein, all such schools have to accept the need for intercultural education. The teaching programmes and syllabuses need to be modified, teachers need to develop their skills and understanding of intercultural education and schools as whole organisations need to work out a full response. It also needs to be said here that hitherto much of the response to the new situation has been left to schools with low status and general reputation—with one notable exception—whereas in the future it will be inevitable that all schools should be involved.

In this general situation, the creation of a new ministry for the education of immigrants ('Gemeenschapsministerie van Onderwijs en Brusselse Aangelegenheden') is a highly significant innovation. It is part of the general political developments at the time of writing (May, 1988) in which political parties confronted with the statistics on the foreign population of Brussels and the proportions of immigrant children in primary schools are turning to the Foyer formula as one of the few systems with any established experience and success in Brussels. Although each project must be sensitive to the needs of a particular school and a specific group of children and parents, it is clear that for the foreseeable future the Foyer Model is assured a place in the education of children in Brussels.

Yet, success also brings risks. It will be important to maintain the tradition of a gradualist approach. The Model does not contain a magic formula. Each case needs to be considered separately and a too rapid generalisation from present experience to wide areas of education in Brussels would be inherently dangerous. Each school, each district is different and, as suggested above, immigration and movement within Brussels is not a static phenomenon. The future of the Foyer Model will be exciting and challenging.

Contributors

Michael Byram (1946) took a degree in Modern and Medieval Languages at the University of Cambridge followed by a doctorate in Danish literature at the same university. After teaching foreign languages in secondary education, he became a Lecturer in Education at the University of Durham. He has done research in minority education and foreign language teaching, and published in both fields, including *Minority Education and Ethnic Survival. Case-study of a German School in Denmark*.

Marcel Danesi is Professor of Applied Psycholinguistics, Italian and Semiotics at the University of Toronto. He is co-director (with Jim Cummins) of the National Heritage Language Resource Unit, Ontario Institute for Studies in Education. Recent publications include *Teaching a Heritage Language to Dialect-Speaking Students* (1986), *Studies in Heritage Language Learning and Teaching* (1988) and *Cervello, linguaggio ed educazione* (1988).

José A. Fernández de Rota y Monter is Professor in Social Anthropology at the University of Santiago de Compostela. **Maria del Pilar Irimia Fernández,** psychologist and speech pathologist, is Principal of the Institute for Special Education 'Santiago Apostol' in La Coruña. They have published books on teaching methodology as practised in a number of different educational centres in Spain. They have also carried out anthropological fieldwork in different gallego-speaking areas.

Among the scientific works published lately by Professor Fernández de Rota are his books *Antropologia de un viejo paisaje gallego* and *Gallegos ante un espejo. Imaginacion antropologica en la Historia*.

Koen Jaspaert (1956) studied Germanic Philology at the University of Leuven in Belgium. He obtained his Ph.D. in Linguistics with a study on the standardisation process of Dutch in Flanders. He is currently employed at Tilburg University, the Netherlands. His main topics of research currently are language shift and language loss with adult immigrants.

Johan Leman (1946) has a licentiate degree in Philosophy, Oriental Philology and History, and a doctorate in Social and Cultural Anthropology from the University of Leuven, Belgium. He is the managing director of the Foyer, a socio-educational centre for immigrants in Brussels, and President of C.W. Laken, a medical and anthropological centre in Brussels. He is also a lecturer at the Centre of Social and Cultural Anthropology of the University of Leuven. He has been studying Mediterranean cultures and immigration since 1974. He is currently supervising several research projects on Italian, Spanish, Moroccan and Turkish immigrants in Belgium. He is the author of *From Challenging Culture to Challenged Culture: The Sicilian Cultural Code and the Socio-Cultural Praxis of Sicilian Immigrants in Brussels.*

Gertrud Lemmens studied language and literature at Tilburg University, where she specialised in language and ethnic minorities. After her studies she evaluated the Foyer bilingual education programme focusing on Dutch as a second language. Currently she is working on various projects concerning multicultural and multilingual education in the Netherlands.

Loredana Marchi (1948) has a licentiate degree in Arts and Letters from the University of Trieste, Italy. In Brussels, she has been doing fieldwork among Italian female immigrants since 1974 and among Arab and Turkish female immigrants since 1979. She is a staff member of the Foyer, director of Dar al Amal, the women's organisation of the Foyer, chairwoman of Cittadinanza Migrante, an Italian association in Brussels, and director of the Italian section of the Italian-Flemish bicultural educational projects in Brussels.

Ludo Smeekens (1956) has a licentiate degree in Educational Sciences from the University of Leuven, Belgium. He is a staff member of Foyer where he has done fieldwork among Moroccan and Turkish adolescents since 1980. He is now responsible for the co-ordination of the bicultural education projects of the Foyer and has published several articles on the subject.

Kathleen Snoeck (1962) obtained her licentiate degree in Educational and Psychological Sciences from the State University of Ghent in 1985. She worked as a researcher at the Department of Anthropology in Ghent for two years on the project 'Culture and Mathematics', focusing on the relationship between spatial thinking, culture and mathematics. In connection with this study she did fieldwork among Turkish immigrant children and worked with foreign university students. She is currently attached to the Foyer within the bicultural education projects.

Index